MW01002098

How Modern Media Destroys Our Minds

How Modern Media Destroys Our Minds

The School of Life

Contents

Introduction

We begin with a vast and somewhat incendiary claim: that the media amounts to one of the great contributors to anxiety, confusion and dread in the modern world; that it is responsible for stoking overwhelming degrees of hatred and distraction; that its business models forces it to exaggerate discord; that our advanced technologies of communication have served to supercharge our tribal impulses, and that our capacity to regain a measure of sanity and serenity now depends on learning to approach the content of much of the media with extreme caution and circumspection.

None of this is—of course—anything we're encouraged to think about by the media itself. While relentlessly drawing our attention to the misdemeanours of others, the one problematic dimension the media does not linger on is its own. It typically normalises its role in our lives. It tries to make it seem reasonable that we might check on its updates ten or thirty times a day, stepping out of a children's birthday party or interrupting a walk with our grandmother to inform ourselves of new topics of outrage and terror. It romanticises the moral character of its corporations. It brazenly tells us that it is a supreme source of insight and knowledge—and aligns itself with the progressive forces of science, democracy and justice.

Though susceptibility to a lot of the media's output may cause us difficulties, it is far from delusional. Rather than heralding the breakdown of our minds, an intense response to what we have heard or read on our screens may be the surest evidence yet that we are highly attuned to reality and authentically worried about our species. Indeed, we might wonder what might be faulty or closed-off in someone who wasn't pushed into fear and despair by what they took in—and what might have gone wrong if they managed to remain indifferent in the face of all the provocations and frenzy on their newsfeeds. What would enable them to read comments below an article or follow the digital hounding of strangers—and to continue with their day unmolested? To be traumatised by mass and social media isn't necessarily a proof of madness; it may be the surest sign yet of having remained (against all odds) a balanced and thoughtful creature.

The media often tries to convince us that it has no capacity whatsoever to harm us—and that it would only be its absence that could ever do so. Our response to this line indicates a deep confusion as to the power of words and images, which we seem simultaneously to think can affect us a lot—and in the end not so much at all. On the one hand, we are boundlessly respectful as to what a few finely rendered square centimetres of canvas can do for our souls. Works of art are accorded a centrally prestigious place in our societies: governments spend millions to house and light them correctly, schoolchildren are bussed in from distant corners to sit respectfully in front of them. A group of 8-year-olds will be told to arrange themselves in a semicircle in (for example) the august halls of the National Gallery of Denmark and to look up at a painting by Vilhelm Hammershøi of a woman alone in a white room on a sunny day—and will be informed (though not in precisely these words) that they are in the presence of transcendent greatness.

The claim isn't too strong. Hammershøi is indeed one of the greatest painters. We should ideally spend a good few moments looking at one of his works every

Vilhelm Hammershøi, *A Room in
the Artist's Home in Strandgade,
Copenhagen, with the Artist's Wife*, 1901.

Do images count?
Or not at all?

day. But we cannot logically have it both ways: either images matter greatly, or they don't very much. And if we assume that they do, then we have to wonder what it must be doing to our spirits to commune on an hourly basis with pictures of mobs, riots, murderers, scandals and disasters. What must be happening to our minds in the face of so much that we are exposed to? We can't make an exception for the so-called good images and dismiss the role of the troubling ones. If pictures can save and enhance us, they must also—by the same measure—be able to depress and disorient us. Some of our perturbations of mind must come down to what we have been too innocently looking at for far too long.

It comes down to a question of how sensitive we might be. It took a long time for us to realise how much children register and feel. For most of history, it was assumed that you could rough up small people without too much consequence; you could shout at them, humiliate them, ignore them and beat them, and their lives would carry on more or less without harm. It took many centuries, millennia indeed, until the true fragility of their spirits was noted. In the middle of the 18th century, in the paintings of Thomas Gainsborough, we catch the first glimpses of a new awareness of the impressionability of children. In a study he made of his daughters from 1756, Margaret—then aged 5—reaches out to touch a white butterfly while her sister Mary (a year older) both restrains her and expresses her own curiosity. We're in no doubt that something very important has just happened in the brief lives of these children, and at the same time, we know that this is no more than the fluttering of the wings of a cabbage white. Not coincidentally, just before the painting was made, Britain and France began fighting what became known as the Seven Years' War (1756–1763), a global conflict that unfolded across five continents in what Winston Churchill termed 'the true first world war'. But Gainsborough was deliberately turning his gaze elsewhere, as if to make the novel suggestion that the difficulties and joys in the lives of children could be as significant as manoeuvrings in high politics or the posturings of statesmen.

We understand now how shy children can be, how distressed they may get by the boisterous laughter of a stranger or a jostling in their environment, how much they need to be left in peace to develop at their own pace and how they should be protected from intrusions that they are too defenceless to handle. But their vulnerability is not theirs alone. In substantial part, we retain it throughout adulthood—except with the added problem that we believe ourselves to be immune to the influence of what we insist on calling 'small things'. Feelings of helplessness, anger, frustration, sadness, guilt and shame get lodged inside us without us being able to notice them, let alone gain relief by communicating them. We don't realise how upset we have been made by a stray remark or a rumour. We suffer with all the intensity of small children while assuming ourselves to be hardy and well-armoured soldiers.

One of the most surprising ideas found in the canonical text of ancient Greek philosophy, *The Republic*, written by Plato around 375 BCE, is the claim that in the ideal state, art should be banned. Plato proposes that playwrights, musicians, sculptors and poets should collectively be shown the door and—if necessary—forcefully instructed to stop working. What might have led this otherwise enlightened and civilised philosopher to make such a proposal, which we associate with draconian regimes and dictators? Why would anyone have a problem with art circulating without impediment? It might have looked as if this idea sprang from a lack of respect for the arts, from a tone-deaf martial philistinism. But far from it. Plato wanted to ban art not because he thought it was an unimpressive medium, but because he was in awe at its capacity to reconfigure our minds.

Thomas Gainsborough,
*The Painter's Daughters
Chasing a Butterfly*, c. 1756.

Illustration of the Theatre of
Dionysus, Athens, Greece, 1890

More than liberal thinkers who blithely incline to leave all wordsmiths and picture makers to themselves out of a background feeling that more or less anything can be witnessed without much impact, Plato understood how significant art could be—and he wasn't merely thinking of pornographic or explicit works; his warnings stretched to encompass the sculptures of Myron and Leochares and the plays of Aeschylus and Euripides.

Plato did not truly believe that his suggestion would ever come to pass: he did not have any well-worked-out plans for censorship. His idea was a provocation—but an extremely important one at that, because it exposes liberal minds to a particular incoherence in their thinking. Banning art, and by extension media, is nowhere on the agenda and will never occur in democracies. Nevertheless, with Plato's warnings in mind, we might consider whether, in the privacy of our own lives, we might not undertake an effort to be more selective about what we read and see—in the name of protecting ourselves from our less helpful impulses and passions. It may simply not be very fruitful for us to spend hours in front of certain stories, getting involved in particular debates or failing to sleep because of panic about distant eventualities. We might practise with ourselves a little of what Plato would have advised: self-censorship. We might, after another evening ruined by something we have read, decide to throw our phone to the far edge of the room (or off a high cliff) and turn our minds elsewhere: to a history book, the mind of a child, an interaction with an old friend or some frescoes painted in the refectory of an Italian convent in the 14th century.

We are relentlessly told that we must stay informed, that we need to live intimately in our own times, that we need to bathe in everything that has happened as soon as it has done so. But these messages are in the end advertising slogans for the mass media rather than recommendations for our well-being—and we have no responsibility to listen to them. Our true duty is to ourselves and our loved ones, to the development of our minds and to the maintenance of calm and sanity.

We need to arm ourselves against the varied toxins placed in our mental bloodstreams by certain sections of mass and social media, and for this, we need to be experts at recognising what we are being injected by, and how. We need to learn to take certain stories apart, and to decode their impact and resonance. We need to see how we may become unbalanced and unkind, blind and partisan, how we can forget about empathy and tolerance and how our vindictive impulses can be inflamed. Sides of the media have had a share in slowly driving us towards madness for a hundred years at least; our education system doesn't stand much of a chance against its onslaughts. We need to take care of ourselves. What follows is a diagnostic tool that can help us to spot some of the media's problematic dimensions early on and take their sting out before we have been too badly afflicted; it is a manual of defence against one of the most popular, and too often still unheralded, dangers of our age.

Part I

Media Illnesses

1 ———————————————————

Passivity

1 —— Despair at our species

It's an obvious point, but as we keep forgetting it, it rewards emphasis: the news is chiefly interested in problems. The only things we are ever really told to notice are the awful things. Something has to go very wrong before a moment becomes a story. When we talk of news, really what we are referring to is the insistent narration of disaster and error. News isn't—as we tend to think—concerned with what has happened; it is a record of what should prove frightening and shocking. When journalists complain of a 'slow news day', what they are deep down lamenting is an occasion when —for a few hours, perhaps on account of a perplexing sluggishness on their part—they have allowed us to briefly imagine that there might be grounds for hope.

The spotlight of the media illuminates not 'reality' but a careful selection of events skewed towards dread-fulness—and arguably generates less of a picture of what the world is 'really' like than that possessed by a medieval ancestor who had never heard of anything that had happened beyond the boundaries of their own village.

Most of the time, news of disasters and tragedy wash over us. But in a certain sort of mood, our defences start to crumble. Maybe we don't get out much, perhaps we've no longer got too many things to feel bullish about close to home. Our vision can narrow. We fail to keep the vast open spaces of nature in mind; we forget about the Andean Plateau and the Great Western Desert. We are just in a small airless room with a very unpleasant selection of characters and everyone is shouting. The disasters can feel insistent and aimed at us. The horrors outside can interlock with the terrors within. We may not be able to resist what we hear about any longer: that we are a tragedy of a species, that we can't overlook anything, that we have no mercy, that we like to wound defenceless people, that the left is as bad as the right, and that the prevailing anger and vengefulness will never end. We may be better 'informed' than we have ever been —but we may also be on the verge of losing our sanity.

We have to insist, as our mood sinks, that the media doesn't find reality; it concocts it. It decides—every day in its newsrooms—what apparently 'happened'. And yet so much happens outside of what happens. If we are to endure, we have to keep the normal, more representative and calmer moments of humanity in our thoughts at all times.

We have to think about the ordinary, 'boring' street that has never been in the news and with any luck never will be. Here there are people struggling and suffering, but no one has to date killed or been killed by anyone. There are losses of temper but no bludgeonings. There are tidy cupboards. A lot of people say sorry when they make a mistake and their apologies are accepted and things move on. Not everyone is filled with recrimination. There are some unhappy marriages but moments of grace and plenty of good humour as well. There are birds and the games of children. There is even a cabbage white or two in spring. This is real life too. There are headlines that never appear in the headlines but that we should write for ourselves: ones about endurance, patience, sweetness, clemency and someone carrying a stranger's suitcase up three flights of stairs in a station despite their own difficulties and unexplored sorrows.

With any luck, our own street
will never be in the news.

Many of us don't have an infinity of reasons to find life
bearable and we can run through them fairly quickly
on a bad day. We don't need, on top of everything else,
to remain in a cage constructed for us by people whose
livelihoods depend on digging up ever renewed sources
of ignominy and pain. We can learn to tell the story of
humanity in our own way, for our own sakes. There is
no inbuilt requirement for us to remain transfixed by
everything that distresses us. We can start to weave
and read a fairer and more bearable version of reality.

CNN World Headquarters,
Atlanta, Georgia, USA.

2 —— Censorship and excess

The media typically justifies its existence by saying
that it is there in order to sniff out, and correct, unfair-
ness and corruption. But in order genuinely to bring
about change, in order to create the groundswell of
popular pressure that would eventually force those in
power to reform institutions and laws, what would really
be required is not merely the odd story here or there
about this or that problem, it would be a sustained,
consistent, systematic focus on the most serious
matters of our times.

And this, in the conditions of the modern media,
is generally what is missing: not by chance, but for
some solidly based reasons. It is rare that a story
manages to stay in the news for longer than a week,
however important it might be—and yet nothing

substantial can change within much less than a year, or more usually a decade or two. The need to alter the subject minute by minute is ingrained within the operating instructions of the media. There has to be a continuous shift of focus; once the most exciting and scandalous aspect of a story has been written up, it's time to move on; nothing can be both old and at the same time important; we are meant to be worried, but always about something new: sexism in parliament, slow broadband in the countryside, a malfunctioning part in a jet engine, vitamins for the under-5s. The slurry of concern is unending yet always shifting.

A modern dictator seeking to throttle an impetus for change would never have to do anything as blatant or as crude as to censor the news. They would just have to guarantee a never-ending flow of jolting news, a constantly rotating panoply of stories about murderers, fashion designers, singers and paedophiles that robbed the audience of any capacity to keep a thread on what it was actually concerned about and what truly affected its chances of fulfilment. They would need to make sure that this audience was drowning in news, that it had more news than it could ever consume, that it could never complain of having been denied access to information while at the same time never being able to make any real sense of the cascade of disconnected facts in which it had been submerged in the last twenty-four hours.

There are far better ways to dull the popular will than through censorship: titillation, distraction, excess and bewilderment are infinitely cleverer tools to ensure that the status quo can remain forever undisturbed. Modern corruption doesn't need to rely on anything as blatant as regulation; it can just argue for more freedom. Those who direct our societies are far too smart to ban news; they just give us ever more of it so that we will lose any ability to see what is really happening.

3 —— Helpless witnesses

The media tells us that we need to know everything because then we will *care*. And when we care, we will be able to change things. It's on this basis that we are told about the raft out at sea in which a 4-year-old refugee drowned, and about the village strafed by helicopter gunships where a primary school was obliterated, and about the government official who made off with a large part of the budget or lost the data. It's because knowing is always good that we are told about the little boy molested by his uncle in a basement over a decade and about the town far away where girls are vaginally mutilated before their 11th birthdays.

The logic sounds starkly sensible, until we fall sick with the classic symptoms of a news-generated illness: a feeling of rage and horror at the iniquities and injustices that we are informed about every day comingled with despair at our wholesale inability to do anything to alleviate them. We are at once appalled and helpless. We know everything and can do precisely nothing.

Knowing and yet doing nothing runs deeply contrary to how we are built. When we hear of a burning building, we are primed to rush upstairs to rescue the imperilled child. When we see someone dragged under the waves, we are designed to want to jump in and try to heave them onto our shoulders.

But the media cares little for this aspect of our natures. It shows us the gravest issues, but it places them behind a very thick pane of glass. We can hear the screams, but we can't make the slightest move to appease them. We are faced by a total rupture between information and agency.

Of course, the media doesn't care for an instant about our disorders; it isn't a nurse. It's concern only extends

Refugees approach the north coast of the
Greek island of Lesbos, 2015. News that
leaves us feeling appalled and helpless.

up to the moment of purchase and engagement. What
we do thereafter is our business, just like a restaurant
that remains nonchalant if we have a coronary out in
the street after one of its rich meals.

We need to bring the information we let into our consciousness more into line with what we can change.
If we cannot do anything, it may truly be better not to
know. The media has been hugely canny in equating
ignorance with selfishness, but not knowing may
in reality presage the very opposite of selfishness.
Spending our days absorbed in dilemmas that we
have no means to affect drains us of energy and the
will to think through problems; and it is precisely this
that makes us inadvertently selfish. We start to have
an impact only when we can focus on people who are
in reach of our actual resources and knowledge.

We need to understand what we can change and
then free our minds sufficiently so that we still have
the energy and hope left to do something.

Photographers documenting
the London Olympics, 2012.

4 —— Numbness

The media operates under the assumption that we will
start to care about an issue as soon as we know that it
is serious and that the facts about it have been outlined
to us. Exactly how we are introduced to it, through what
specific words or images, with what care and aesthetic
merit, isn't taken to be the point: brute knowledge will
—it is assumed—be enough to generate concern.

In truth, what contributes to the impact of any story is
not so much the content as the way this is imparted.
There are ways of narrating dramatic events that
drain them of any impression of significance; there
are writers and photographers who could make a

world war feel a bit dull. And at the same time, there are wordsmiths and picture makers of genius who can grip us with their narration of a quiet conversation in a kitchen between a mother and her son or move us to tears by a photograph of the last beams of the evening sun illuminating a vase on a window ledge.

This is the insight upon which a belief in art is built. What qualifies someone as a great artist isn't any kind of predefined subject matter, it is the way they go on to handle it. A great book won't automatically emerge from an eventful story, and many a masterpiece has hung on events as delicate and invisible as a spider's web.

The news, partly because it sits on top of the most overtly 'large' stories that ever occur, has seldom taken this idea much to heart. We often end up in the bewildering situation where we hear that 10,000 people have lost their homes in a conflict—and do not feel a thing; where numbers are paraded before us (about how many are unemployed or are having trouble with discrimination) and we sigh and move on. The media assumes that if it bombards us with sufficient information about important events, we will care. And yet indifference and apathy can't be overcome by information alone; it can only be vanquished through art.

In November 1807, readers of the *Times* in London or the *Zürcher Zeitung* in Zurich would have been able to read another story about Napoleon Bonaparte's aggressive attempts to reconfigure European politics. The dictator had just ordered 23,000 French troops into Spain and set about trying to replace the royal family and turn the country into a de facto French colony. At first, the Spanish nobility cooperated with the invaders, but opposition slowly grew, and by the 2nd May 1808, an uprising began in Madrid, with rioters burning French flags and attacking soldiers. As newspapers reported, the French, led by Marshal

Murat, responded harshly and had many of the rebels rounded up, thrown into prison and put to death. It was sad no doubt, but you would have had to be unusually sensitive—eating lunch in a rectory in Hampstead or a lakeside villa in Bellevue—to neglect for long the next bite of mackerel or rösti for this sort of news. Such events happen pretty much every day in one form or another somewhere around the world—and no one normally cares for very long. The blood is mopped up and the caravan of humanity moves on. But luckily for the rebels and for posterity, someone else was watching with a power far greater than that of most journalists. The 62-year-old Spanish painter Francisco Goya was in Madrid and turned the events into one of the most significant and moving protests against violence and state-sanctioned cruelty ever rendered. In his *The Third of May, 1808*, a group of French soldiers have their muskets trained on a desperate rebel who has only seconds left to live. He is anguished, pitiful and pleading for his life; next to him, the corpses of his compatriots lie in a heap, leaking blood across the earth. The sky is dark with foreboding; other rebels —soon to be killed in turn—shield their eyes from the unfolding abomination.

Most of us have long stopped caring about the news of a five-year Peninsular War between the Spanish and the French, but Goya's painting resonates as a cry of pain across the centuries. It continues to argue against cruelty and to beseech us to access our humanity and pity. As the American poet and critic Ezra Pound understood, art is news that stays news.

Great artists are able to tease out significance in events that we had never imagined could remotely count as a story or point of interest. Such was Goya's talent, he could show us a pile of dead fish—and suddenly, without even knowing we cared about the fate of golden bream, we could be moved by their

Francisco Goya, *The
Third of May, 1808*, 1814.

Francisco Goya, *Still Life with
Golden Bream*, c. 1808–1812.

brutal end and the underlying price of our appetites;
we could stare into their sad relatable faces, and realise
—perhaps for the first time—that we hadn't just bought
ourselves some dinner, we had been accessories to
a murder.

The media cannot accept that bare information isn't
on the whole sufficient. We know quite well that there
is something called poverty in Bangladesh and illit-
eracy in South Sudan. We realise that many children in
all countries have hard lives. But we're not moved by
such abstractions. We don't care that unemployment
in Greece is seventeen per cent, that the average wage
in Burundi is US$7,890 per annum, that there were
232,000 car thefts in France last year, that twenty-eight
per cent of boys in the UK aged between 8 and 16 say
they enjoy reading compared with sixty-two per cent
of girls. Our respect for data is fed by the tempting but
false idea that 'knowing the facts' will change our minds.
But facts tend to wash over us. As Goya understood.

There is a further mistake that the media makes in
trying to get us interested in tragedy. It tells us about
the gore, the bombs, the landslides, the murders and
the calamities. The focus is relentlessly on the shocking
and the bloody. But in reality, when a troubled bit of the
earth is seen as deeply and permanently awful, news of
yet more outrages and horrors has ever less impact on
us. It just confirms a bleak belief that a region is beyond
all reason and redemption already.

Countries can be made to disappear into their worst
moments; through the media, they become merely
suicide bombers and tanks, epidemics and wailing
mothers. But the route to caring about the extraordinary is through the ordinary. We need to feel close to
the normal moments of others' lives before we can care
about what might happen to them in their tragedies.
This is what makes work like that of the Jordanian

photojournalist Tanya Habjouqa arresting. Unlike most photojournalists operating in the Middle East, who show us hackneyed imagery of, for example, Palestinians as either proponents or victims of violence in the West Bank and Gaza, Habjouqa trains her lens on different elements; she looks at what is fun, charming, sweet and deeply normal in one of the most troubled parts of the world.

When we see Habjouqa's images of girls in Ramallah preparing for a dance, we are moved and reassured that the attractions of dancing and high heels are not going to be extinguished by conflict—and so we are all the more ready to feel the importance of peace. Our foreign press photographers should show us not just what is ghastly, but also—as importantly—what remains inspiring and kind. Despite their astonishing technical capabilities, we know so little about ordinary life in deprived lands; we don't know whether anyone has ever had a normal day in the Democratic Republic of the Congo, for no such thing has ever been recorded by a Western news organisation; we have no idea what it's like to go to school or visit the hairdresser in Haiti; it's entirely mysterious whether anything like a good marriage is possible in Somalia; and we are equally in the dark about office life in Turkmenistan and what people do on the weekend in Algeria. The ideal news organisation of the future, recognising that an interest in the anomalous depends on a prior knowledge of the normal, would tell us about street parties in Addis Ababa, love in Peru, in-laws in Mongolia and barbecues in Nablus, so that audiences could be prepared to care just a little more about the next devastating typhoon, coup, cluster bomb or outbreak of haemorrhagic fever.

——————
Tanya Habjouqa, *Occupied
Pleasures*, 2013.

A news story may stir us
deeply; but for how long?

5 —— Sentimentality

In his essay *De Profundis*—written in prison after his ostracism and disgrace—Oscar Wilde defined sentimentality as the desire to feed off an emotion 'without paying for it'. 'We think we can have our emotions for nothing,' he wrote. 'We cannot. Even the finest and most self-sacrificing emotions have to be paid for.'

What does it mean to want to feed off an emotion 'without paying for it'? It points us to the idea that many emotions are distinctly gratifying to experience—joy, loyalty, desire, even outrage, fury and self-righteousness. However, emotions rightly entail commitments that are less pleasant to have to honour. For example, we may want to know the feeling of being forgiven, but we often don't want to say sorry. We want to be admired, but we don't want to be especially good. We want the bracing sensation of hating someone intensely, but we can't be bothered to find out whether they really did something wrong. Or consider the way that we sometimes look for someone to be our friend without wanting to pay the actual price of friendship. We want the respect, the warmth and the feeling of being the target of kindness. But we don't want to back up the other person when they are in difficulties, we don't want to hear about their romantic problems or give them tricky bits of advice. We don't actually want to do the things that real friends do. We just want the warm glow when we invite them to lunch (at a non-specific date) or emphasise that they can always count on us and add that they only have to ask, knowing full well that they will never dare—and that we wouldn't help them even if they did cry out.

The media renders us sentimental because it daily excites us to have feelings that we haven't earned the right to have and cannot legitimately inhabit; it convinces us that we care deeply about the fate of a little boy with cancer who only has days left to live, but three weeks later, we can't remember the poor child's name, let alone his end. We start to cry about what happened to a young girl maltreated by her parents and tell our partner how lovely her hair and eyes were in all the pictures the press unfurl for us (especially one of her on her first day at school), but soon enough, we've overcome our pain and lost any memory of who this creature actually was. The disparity between the depth of emotion an occasion would properly demand and our own brief burst of feeling does a disservice to reality and comes close to obscene; as if we had dropped in for a pleasant little cry on the saddest day of someone else's life or had made off with the cakes at a funeral. We are continuously taken into moments of loss or excitement and made to experience ourselves as intimates —when we are in reality just pausing momentarily on an endless voyeuristic safari. We're sure that we are horrified by the treatment of young calves or the underfunding of schools for minorities, by the sex scandal of the politician or the money stolen by the executive—and for a few days, we're genuinely worked up. But nothing sticks. We won't remember anything about our tears, our longings, our fury and our cardboard commitments to agitate for change. We'll go to the vigil and sign our names on a register, but by year's end, we won't have a clue what it was about.

The fault isn't ours; we are given such a meagre basis on which to found our commitments and mould our values. Our minds are being played with, tickled here, prodded there, by people who care only that we keep responding, not that any of our reactions make sense or are anchored in substantial soil. Guided by the media, this attitude threatens to spread from our response to stories in the news to our behaviour in our own lives. Educated by what we have consumed, we may start to become people who too quickly believe that they are moved, or committed to a cause, who too rapidly say that something is shocking or the sweetest thing ever—when they are merely deriving pleasure from a rolling succession of momentary emotional highs.

We should learn to husband our emotions more carefully. In response to particular corruptions, we might quietly remark that we can't be outraged because it's none of our business to be so and that we don't really understand a story in the depths required to care properly. Or in relation to an invitation to hate someone, we might say that we won't—because we don't know enough about how we ourselves might have acted had we been in their place. Or we might insist that we can't weep about a crime because we never knew the victim, and that we won't call the dead child by their first name or look at their teddy because she was no relative of ours. To remain people who can still feel real things, we might more regularly have to feel nothing.

2

Celebrity

1 —— The fame game

From a distance, becoming famous seems like the natural and logical solution to the problems of existence. We will at last have enough money; people will take us seriously. We'll go on tropical holidays. We won't have to worry about finding a partner. Strangers will be impressed by our name alone. The normal humiliations will disappear.

Fame is liable to be of particular appeal to those who have suffered unduly in their lives, people who have been bullied at school, haunted by poverty or mistreated by their parents. No one would want to be known to millions who hadn't at some point gone through some exceptional periods of neglect. Conversely, the clearest sign of being a good and watchful parent is that your child has no wish whatsoever to get into the public eye.

And yet—as the media, the principal creator of fame, artfully never tells us—fame can't possibly accomplish what we ask of it—and indeed it inevitably perpetrates the very opposite. Every new famous person who disintegrates in public, who abuses drugs, acts erratically, breaks down on stage or babbles incoherently on late-night television is interpreted as a rarity, rather than being pitied as the inevitable next victim of the grinder of renown.

We want to be famous for one principal and poignant reason: because we are looking to be treated with kindness. But the audience is never predisposed to be kind to famous people for very long. They may be charmed by them at first, but they soon find reason to complain: their songs aren't as good as they used to be, they shouldn't have got divorced, they're starting to look out of shape, their sexuality seems to be a bit stranger than feels decent. At the same time, the benefits of fame serve to excite the reserves of envy of the most deprived segments of the public: why do the famous have so many houses, why do they travel on board such expensive planes? It doesn't seem in any way fair, and so, to restore an element of justice, the onlookers start to gripe about their now fraudulent-seeming heroes, they leave vicious comments below articles about them, spread rumours and maybe (drunk late at night) send them a direct message or two telling them to die.

Soon enough, the famous person finds themselves in a vortex of paranoia. They are known to all, they cannot leave the house without being photographed, but the respect and kindness that they hoped for is ebbing. There are rumours and jokes online. The newspaper that gave them a pleasant interview a few years back is now running stories about their finances and making harsh remarks about their behaviour on dates. Old so-called friends have told journalists things they shouldn't. Every element of a scandal is kept perma-nently in circulation by the unforgiving surveillance system of the internet.

The famous are especially unable to take any of this. They may not have been totally well to begin with and now they're uncommonly unfit to cope with the downsides of a poor reputation. They can't shrug off 'what other people think'; it's been their life's mission to care very closely about their image in others' eyes. They can't simply 'love themselves'; they were looking to the crowd to appease their self-hatred. They can't take pride in their achievements; they have no capacity for self-worth. And so, they descend into addiction and crisis as a way of giving shape to what is tearing them apart inside and of begging the world to stop emphasising how despicable they are.

The only escape is to recognise that fame was never an answer to the problems that inspired the longing for it. The interest of strangers can never compensate for the close and loving attention of a few thoughtful people. The true solutions to the problems of loneliness and shame lie in friendship, a sensitive therapist with whom to process the worst parts of our childhood and anonymity—a philosophy that the media opts to never share with us, preferring to watch yet another generation of hopeful and troubled young people scale the mountain of fame and die on its windswept granite cliff face.

The most effective morality tale about fame is to be found in the contrasting destinies of two of the most famous pop stars of the 1980s. For a long time, one was known to have remained a success, the other to have morphed into an almost comically thorough failure. Alongside his friend George Michael, Andrew Ridgeley was for a few years one part of the world's most successful pop duo.

But after Wham! split, Ridgeley's public career fell apart: he tried acting, car racing and a solo album. But nothing came of the efforts, and Ridgeley eventually moved to an old farmhouse in a remote part of Cornwall with his partner of many years, Keren Woodward, who had been in the girl group Bananarama. He learnt to play golf. His hair fell out. He went to the pub, he got involved in local causes and he worried about sewage being pumped into the sea.

George Michael and Andrew Ridgeley,
1980s. The members of Wham! at the
height of their music career.

It grew natural to think of Andrew as a failure. He
had fallen off the stage of stardom; he was no longer
pictured outside nightclubs; he was the guy who had
been famous; he liked the local fish and chips—whereas
George Michael continued to gleam in the erratic
diamond lights of public esteem.

But with George Michael now interred beneath a flower-
strewn grave in Highgate Cemetery, we are in a better
position to see that it might in fact have been Andrew
who had learnt to be successful in the true sense of
the term; that is, who had understood how to achieve
contentment in the bounds of his own being and reconciled himself to the dimensions of reality. He had
grasped how to replace the adulation of the crowd

Andrew Ridgeley, London, 2019.
The true success of ordinariness.

with the kindly attentions of a partner and a handful of loyal friends. He had opted to no longer compensate for early deprivation by hunting out the interest of strangers. He had stopped worrying what was being said about him online. He had come to live according to his own values rather than those insisted upon by the media. Against many odds, he had made it.

We should dare to follow Ridgeley on the path to contented anonymity. Fame will never give us what we need. It is a phantom created by the media—designed to shield us from what we secretly aspire to find: the friendship of a small group of kindly souls who can help to heal our griefs and will nightly gather with us in a local pub for a few hours of affectionate conversation.

2 —— The pain of meritocracy

We know the story very well by now. It has a few local variations, but its essence remains identical. One or two seemingly very normal people, not especially successful at school, never part of the in-group or attractive to potential partners, had a bright idea. No one quite believed in them at first, they were just a geeky duo with strange hair and a business plan. They were close to their mums and went kite surfing on the weekend. But then a couple of investors got curious and took a punt, just a few hundred thousand at this stage, but that was enough for them to rent a garage in a run-down part of town and hire a handful of coders. Shortly after, they sold their first big contract. Word spread among clients. No one could get enough of what they were offering. It was such a marked advance on what anyone else had thought of. Within half a year, revenues were at the six-million-dollar mark. Four months later, they had gone up three hundred per cent. Now they've been at it for two years and—though still only just past thirty—they are each worth twelve, or it might be fourteen, billion dollars; it depends on how things are valued and how the upcoming IPO goes.

We're meant to be delighted for them—and in a way we are. They are obviously lovely people. And they remain hugely down to earth as well. They aren't going to lord it over anyone. They still wear T-shirts. They are still friends with old pals from home. They're not going to rub it in your face that their wealth exceeds the combined GDP of a handful of sub-Saharan African nations.

Nevertheless, we can't deny it, we are crushed—and in a particularly modern and media-generated way. The nub of the humiliation is that they were once so much like us—and are now so obviously out of this world. It's the particular shift from ordinariness to distinctiveness that underpins our envy and despair.

The founders of the financial
services company Stripe.

Unknown artist, *Dudley, Third
Baron North (1581–1666)*, c. 1615.

In the olden days, people of wealth and power were obviously different from us from the start. They inherited long and complicated names, their accents were odd, they went to elite schools, they drove around in golden carriages, they had top hats and glorious suits of armour.

More importantly, they were born to privilege they hadn't earned and so didn't really deserve. We might have wanted their advantages, but their wealth didn't reflect badly on our own poverty. We could hate them with impunity from a distance—and their castles and servants did not affect our self-esteem. The world was obviously rigged, the rich didn't deserve their status —and we evidently weren't to blame for our mediocrity.

But the modern world has stripped us of our ability to tell ourselves comforting stories about our positions. We are meant to be the authors of our own destinies. No longer should lineage or background hold us back; we are allowed to compete in fair and open races. Our winners are worthy because they began at the same level as everyone else, which means that our losers must, by the same token, also deserve their fates. Through the media, we are continuously exposed to examples of people who began life at the bottom and then triumphed. Their advantages cannot, as in ages past, be put down to kleptocracy or luck—and our relative failure cannot be excused as a symptom of an unfair class system. The question of why, if we have any claim to talent or virtue, we remain on the bottom rung has become a personally painful question in a meritocratic, news-soaked era.

We should take heed when turning to the business sections with their inevitable accounts of young people in T-shirts smiling broadly. These are the sort of tales that could, in a fragile mood, cut our lives short. If the media were kind, it would signal at the end of yet another admiring profile that we have ample permission to feel complicated about others' success.

@thelipstickfever
Instagram account.

Media Illnesses

3 —— FOMO

The one thing that media of all kinds can always agree
on is that the life we are currently leading is the wrong
one. There are other sorts of shoes (more pointed ones)
we should be wearing, there are other destinations
we should be visiting (ones with cabanas) and other
opinions (less unconsciously biased ones) we should
be holding. They leave us in no doubt about just how
much we have missed out on; intense and painful doses
of FOMO (Fear of Missing Out) are their stock-in-trade.

There are, fundamentally, two ways in which the brute
facts of missing out can be viewed: we can take either
a Romantic or a Classical approach. To the Romantic
temperament, there is no alternative but to suffer,

to long and to seek to become someone different. Somewhere else, noble, interesting and progressive people are living exactly the lives that should be ours. We would be happy, if only we could be working in that debt-relief agency off Washington Square, holidaying in that lodge in Costa Rica or putting in time in a recording studio in Kingston. Romantics trust in the idea of a defined centre where the most rewarding activities must be occurring. At one time, the centre was New York, for a few years it was Berlin, then Milan. Now, it is probably Portland, and in five years it could be Santiago—or perhaps Fez or Baden-Württemberg. For the Romantic, humanity is divided into a large group of the mediocre—and a tribe of the elect, numbering DJs, mural artists, the edgy part of the aid world and those launching an eco-friendly brand of lipliner or moccasin.

By contrast, how drab and resigned the ordinary can be. Our mother, its chief representative, is capable of driving us to despair: her life is from certain angles terrifying in its greyness and acceptance. Why can't she see the structures of power in which she is implicated and of which she is a victim? She is always suggesting we see the upsides of our job and inviting us on walking holidays in the Lake District. She likes to point out that all lives have their drawbacks and that few things are black and white. Sometimes we have been rather rude to her. We avoid certain people like the plague: the shy friend from school who refuses to post on social media; the flatmate who became a vet and learns German on weekends. Being around individuals who are so lacking in ambition and awareness can feel fatal.

For their part, classically minded people acknowledge that there are of course some genuinely special and important things going on in the world, but they doubt that the impatient hallmarks of value as put out by the media are a good guide to finding them. The best novel in the world, they like to think, is probably not currently winning prizes or garnering admiring profiles on prominent blogs. It may be being written at this moment by an arthritic elderly ex-schoolteacher living in the otherwise unremarkable Latvian town of Liepāja —and will be published with no fanfare and few reviews in a decade or two.

Classical people keep in mind that good qualities tend to coexist alongside very ordinary ones. Everything is confusingly jumbled up. Old-fashioned political views are compatible with real insight. Academic qualifications can give no indication of true intelligence. Famous people can be dull. Obscure ones can be remarkable. At the launch of a manifesto, drinking sandalwood cocktails in the basement of an old foundry, we can feel sad and anxious, yet we might have the deepest conversations of our life with our aunt—even though she likes watching snooker on television and has stopped dying her hair.

The classical temperament fears on missing out as well, but it has a different list of things it is afraid of letting slip by: getting to truly know our parents, learning to cope well with being alone, appreciating the consoling power of trees, discovering a new kind of cinema, chatting to a 7-year-old, exchanging views with someone we feared, surrendering certainty ... We can indeed miss out on extremely important things, but the danger is never higher than when we have allowed the media to taunt and convince us that life must, always and necessarily, be elsewhere.

4 —— The redemption of the ordinary

Very occasionally, completely by chance, something very special and oddly joyful happens. While pursuing famous people around the world, the media will catch one of them doing something extremely normal. For example, going to the supermarket for some groceries. It might be some lettuce or pasta, perhaps some cans of tomatoes or a few packs of kitchen roll—we can't quite tell from the photos. The media would surely have preferred if the celebrity were dressed up in a gown by Balenciaga on their way to an award party or stepping out of a helicopter in St Moritz, but a picture of a star is always worth something, so it gets published anyway. And without quite knowing why, we are mesmerised and not a little delighted and redeemed by what we see.

Our relief and pleasure tells us something important about the pain of living in highly stratified societies dominated by the media's glamourising strategies. These serve to split the world into two cruelly opposed categories: a higher realm where special people live, eating special foods, wearing special clothes, doing special things, travelling in special ways. And a normal world where normal people like us live, doing normal things and struggling along in normally banal ways.

This stratification inspires heavy doses of alienation and self-hatred. What is close to hand starts to feel inherently demeaning and wrong. Nothing that we do can possibly be as good as what the other, blessed category are up to.

Yet when famous people are spotted in the aisles of grocery stores, a different message comes through, a message about how our own lives might be decent enough and worth focusing on and deriving pleasure from, because even people who have options will —at points—want to do exactly as we do.

Rihanna shopping at Whole
Foods, New York City, 2012.

No one is forcing a world-famous singer or actor to go
to the supermarket; they do it because it's a useful and
quick response to the challenges of eating well (they
can see just what's available and be reminded of a few
things they hadn't thought of). It can also be beautiful
to see the products neatly lined up under clean bright
lights—and a relief to get out of the house for a while.

One of the greatest moves ever made by a world
religion was Christianity's decision to locate the birth
and upbringing of its central deity in highly ordinary
circumstances. It was a stroke of genius to give Jesus
ordinary parents and a very normal start (other religions
had until then endowed their holy figures with only the
noblest sorts of lineage). The birth in a barn, the car-
pentry, the village life, these helped to heal the division
between the realms of the ordinary and the anointed.

Taylor Swift shopping at Bristol
Farms, Los Angeles, 2013.

Queen Elizabeth II looks around a
Waitrose supermarket during a visit
to Poundbury, Dorchester, 2016.

They showed that grace was available to all at every level. Holiness could exist in humble surroundings, in a modest kitchen or around a not perfectly finished house. As a result, we could come to consider our own lives without instinctive disdain; we didn't just have to endure what we had been allotted, we were not alone; we could know that we had the very same sort of life that the king of kings had chosen to lead.

In a secularised form, the very same message is being sent to us when a celebrity is photographed by the lettuces. In such cases too, we are being reminded that our lives may not be as awful as we had supposed, that they may have elements to them that even the most powerful of beings would willingly choose to partake in—and that we don't therefore have to hate ourselves as intensely as we thought. The media may not quite realise what it is doing, but it is—through its occasional incidental shots of stars with laden trolleys—helping to repair the damage it has caused and nudging us to recover faith in our own circumstances and choices.

Nastiness

1 —— Monsters

One thing that unites media organisations from around the world is their conviction that their principal and most valuable contribution to society lies in their ability to track down and expose monsters. A monster is a very special category of human in this context and is held to share eight principal features: (i) they perpetrate evil entirely on purpose, (ii) they can never be stopped politely or kindly, (iii) they have to be shamed, (iv) they can never be reformed, (v) they had no childhood that explains anything (in a way, they had no childhood at all), (vi) they harbour no remorse, (vii) they can never be pitied, and (viii) they are fundamentally and quasi-anatomically different from you or me, breathing as they do an alternative and monstrous air, having monstrous curdled blood in their capillaries and having been born —probably during a full moon—under a sign of Satan to the howling of wolves.

Very occasionally in the history of the media, it has happened that a true monster has been found: perhaps in the office of the president, or in an army division or a suburban basement. And from such extraordinary and seismic discoveries, which might number no more than a handful across any century, a general belief has taken hold in every single media organisation and in the minds of every last aspiring journalist: that there are monsters everywhere, in offices, homes, gyms, airport control towers, operating theatres and cabinet rooms.

Luis Bárcenas, former treasurer of Spain's
People's Party, after being accused of tax
evasion and money laundering, 2013.

These monsters can be split up by type: there are
capitalist monsters, environmental monsters, tech
monsters, school monsters, political monsters, sex
monsters (a particular favourite) and racist monsters
—all of them just waiting to be uncovered with skill and
tenacity by professional monster-hunters and photographed, bleary eyed, opening the door to a pack of
journalists at dawn and asked to make a comment on
their unfathomable monstrosity, a small frightened
offspring-of-monster child perhaps just visible
cowering in the background.

The media sticks tightly to the script. Monsters are
an active menace, and the only way to deal with them
is through unrelenting sweeps of the territory by their
well-trained operatives. Only thereby can society be

protected and the innocent sleep safely at night. It's a comforting-sounding tale and inevitably an entirely self-serving and in its own way properly monstrous one as well. The more complicated reality is that, as psychoanalysts have been trying to teach us with little success for a century or more, there are no monsters; there are only certain extremely damaged people who act in desperate ways to give external form to inner anguish—and are in urgent need not of prison and hate, but treatment and care.

We know too, from our own lives not least, that people ache to change, even those—especially those—who have done something very wrong. The moment the frenzied murder is over, many a killer will hold up their bloodstained hands and implore the heavens to correct what they have just done; the embezzler or sexual criminal will sit in their cell for three decades regretfully turning over how they let their passions overwhelm them; the crooked politician will beseech the authorities for a chance to turn over a new leaf. And when we ourselves have shouted and said appalling things late at night to someone we love, we want nothing more than an opportunity to be someone different tomorrow.

We know deep down that change never comes when people are humiliated. It is not by branding someone a pervert or a weirdo and placing their name in the digital public register for an eternity that they ever become one jot saner or safer to be around. The monster-hunters fear that no good will ever come from forgiveness and that mercy must be for the weak—but the strength of a society can be measured not by its enthusiasm for punishing and chastising but by the depths of its reserves of clemency and magnanimity.

2 —— Schadenfreude

There is a complicated truth behind our nastiest impulses: we are nasty chiefly because we're unhappy. The paradox is that if only we could understand this about ourselves, and forgive ourselves for the origins of our hard-heartedness, then we would have the energy to do good—and could, in time, have so much less to be unhappy about. But for now, it seems far easier to cheer on the destruction of others' lives and take satisfaction from sackings, scandals and the most dreadful court cases.

We can catch an inkling of our lust for misery at work in an apparently disconnected and unusual area: our attitudes to hurricanes and winter storms. The strange truth is that we like these extreme weather systems enormously—as the media well know. We love it when, towards the middle of September, the first of the tropical depressions build in the mid-Atlantic and start to mass and whirl off the Gulf of Mexico. We can hardly wait to see the shutters blowing off stores in downtown areas and National Guards talking of the dangers of broken levees and downed power lines. By February, we are equally gripped by the possibility of a complete shutdown of all schools, workplaces and transport centres. We love to see metres of snow piled up at railway sidings and to watch airliners—once proud and relentless —lying prostate like smashed toys across icy runways.

It satisfies something deep in us to see so much chaos. Apparent creatures of order, we appear to have a lot of time for images of doom. The reason may come down to how silently unfulfilling our own neat lives are. We take pride, day-to-day, in our spotless kitchens, laundry cupboards and account books, but really, in our hearts, something aches for more: for love, heroism, sincerity, a chance of a new beginning. Our world can feel like a prison and we secretly want to put a bomb under our

Heavy snow storms delay flights
at John F. Kennedy International
Airport, New York City, 2018.

quiet misery and start afresh. That's why we don't really
mind the storm at all. It could dump fifteen metres of
snow on us and might offer us a chance to burrow out
and discover new ways to be.

Mostly though, storms pass without destroying too
much. Order returns, the cyclone relents, the ice melts.
But still the ache within us persists and seeks fresh
targets for its dissatisfactions. And here the media is
on hand. There may not be a meteorological cataclysm

available at all times, but what can reliably be served up almost every day is evidence of yet another human being imploding. It might be a sex scandal, an outburst of violence, an ill-judged phone call, a sudden sacking —something to bring down someone who was once elevated and mighty and (inadvertently) made us feel small and inconsequential.

How we enjoy the winds blowing through their life. We follow how they are dragged from home, bundled into an SUV and taken to the courthouse for an initial hearing about the shocking allegations. We hear a confused neighbour, who borrowed a lawnmower from them only a week ago, explain that they never suspected this of them. We love the storm of outrage and follow the pitiful suspect weeping for forgiveness in front of a pack of taunting journalists.

On other days, we adore looking at pictures of how once beautiful people have been gnawed by time or study how lottery winners have evaporated their winnings at gambling tables. There's fun to be found in following the hurricanes of infidelity shattering once-beatific marriages or in learning of a formerly influential pop star now living forgotten and penniless in a shack in the wilds, in rereading the embarrassing messages the adulterer sent to their lover or in hearing how the proud head of a film studio had to resign after a storm of allegations by an intern. Without quite real- ising it, we have become truly failed people—that is, people who need other people to fail.

The solution, as ever, is not to condemn us but to be extremely compassionate for the many reasons why the downfall of others provides us with so much relief. We are not evil, we are simply—far more than we know—deeply unhappy. We shouldn't be brutally ordered never to experience schadenfreude again, we should be allowed to explore what made us so angry

Matthew Perry photographed
in 2000 (left) and 2017 (right).

Lindsay Lohan arrives for a hearing
at the Beverly Hills Courthouse, 2010.

and so sad in the first place, why the world appears to us to have let us down so badly—and why we now need everything to go wrong for strangers.

We should be allowed to mourn that we do not look as nice as we had hoped, that we have not earned the money we wanted and that no one has properly recognised our talents or our potential. We should be allowed to complain that it isn't fair and have someone gently take us in their arms and repeat in a gentle voice 'I know, I know' while they stroke our brow with patience and tenderness.

To wean us off our bitter delight, we require not sermons, but help to lead lives that do not feel so regret-filled and forlorn. We will be in a position to be a little less excited by disaster when—at last—we are no longer so alone and unconsoled.

3 —— Sanctimony

We can hardly withhold our disgust. Apparently, on what was meant to be a business trip, a trip paid for by us, the taxpayers, ostensibly justified by the need to help some of the world's neediest people, after six hours of plenary meetings and a hard-won agreement on a draft agenda, the official slipped out, gave his security guards the night off, and headed to a part of town that shouldn't even exist. The rest—as the media tells us in horror—is simply appalling. She wasn't much more than 20; his wife recently gave birth to twins; he may even have been a churchgoer.

It may be challenging, of course, but in a more compli-cated and psychologically mature world, we wouldn't feel the need to condemn as avidly as we do. We would be able to admit how much our loathing is driven by impulses we know from the inside but have not been able to discuss even with ourselves. No one could be as cross and as morally indignant as we are who wasn't—somewhere inside—also a bit turned on.

We should have the courage to explore how much part of us longs to be gagged and bound, or alternatively beaten and whipped; how much we too have sometimes gone to some unusual places in our imaginations, where —for a few moments—we reached a pitch of ecstasy doing things we might want to kill ourselves for if any-one knew. Even as we look at certain photos that ask us to have only one sort of sensible response, a tiny wayward part of us is off having another: there is a strand in us that wants to lick and caress the innocent or offer ourselves to the bully or insult the victim or defend the perpetrator or put on the tights or the suit of the criminal. In short, it's all—in private—far, far more complicated.

A society is civilised to the extent that it can find room in its collective imagination for some of this complexity—and reins in the sanctimonious fury of those who cannot accept their own natures. Such a society would recognise that we can remain good parents and honourable citizens and yet still have some very intense and surprising daydreams.

4 —— Solutions

It looks as if they want to make it better; that's why they are telling us about the racism, that's why they are exposing the low wages, that's why they remind us again and again about the bullying.

But we should keep a darker point in view; the media need this conflict far more than we do. If they didn't, there would be so many other ways to proceed. They could get curious about why the problem had come about, they could allow for atonement, they wouldn't need to set the price of apology impossibly high, they would behave like loving parents do when children have strayed.

Instead, they give themselves away through their remorselessness; when it might be time to calm a situation down, they return with manic energy to the original offence; when there might be an opportunity for solutions, they keep giving voice to those who are unreconciled and furious.

The entire business model is premised on walking past solutions. It doesn't look like it (they are clever enough to cover their tracks), but they have zero interest in couples no longer hitting one another, they absolutely don't want race relations to improve, they don't want workplaces to be harmonious, they don't want capitalism to function, they don't want any wise accommodation between employers and employees, they don't want countries to be at peace, they don't want riots to cease and they certainly don't want the environment to be—on balance—OK.

Their lifeblood is unhappiness. They will have a job only so long as we continue to squabble and to wound. They are the enemies of what they claim to seek for us. We should be in no doubt how little on our side they truly are.

The arrest of Malcolm Fairley,
aka 'The Fox', in London, 1984.

Charles, Prince of Wales, and Camilla,
Duchess of Cornwall, talking quietly
together during a visit to Wales, 2018.

5 —— Secrets

One of the media's most common and favoured moves is to render what was once private public—and to frame the step as an act of morality. Despite the mortification and lifelong embarrassment of those who have been exposed, we are invited to think that justice has been served and humanity uplifted through the divulgations. After all, the private is the realm of darkness, corruption and untoward dealings—and only under the bright lights of the media can justice flourish and goodness have its day. We should, in a perfect world, live in glass houses.

That's why the media has no qualms eavesdropping on conversations, republishing texts, turning private memos into headlines and letting the whole world know about what was once believed to be only for two lovers in a bedroom or a set of closely knit colleagues in a boardroom.

It sounds almost sensible, until we remember just how much we ourselves depend on secrets in order to survive. The blanket assertion that secrets are shameful fails to reckon with the facts of our natures and the nuances of our experience. We know that there are people we love who could not take the full truth. We know that there are thoughts that, though necessary, would hurt unbearably if they were shared candidly. There is so much we need to say that would be prone to misinterpretation. There are moments when we need to vent things that don't reflect our considered beliefs but that need to be uttered in fury so that we can subsequently make peace with our more nuanced positions. And for this, we need times when the microphones are off, when we can be certain that our words will never be passed on and when we can have confidence that no one is slipping in a screenshot.

The media dignify nosiness with the word scrutiny; they call it public accountability; they call it honesty. But really it is a primitive joy at causing a powerful or significant person mortification. There is apparent rectitude in wielding the word hypocrite, but hypocrisy is a precondition of a benevolent existence. The good functioning of our lives relies on maintaining a distinction between what is thought and what is said, what is circulated to a few and what is known to many.

We should learn to celebrate those rare times when we are left wholly in the dark, when we are denied access to diaries, when there are no memoirs to be read or documents to be downloaded off a hacked server, when private papers are burnt and when someone goes to the grave with a quixotic smile after having repeatedly turned down fortunes from publishers—because they have understood the necessity and moral dignity of secrecy.

Wang Baoqiang and Ma Rong
at the screening of *Tian Zhu Ding*
at Cannes Film Festival, 2013.

6 —— Gossip

From an early age, kindly people are liable to leave us in no doubt that gossiping about the private lives of well-known or prestigious people is despicable. At the same time, as our search histories and clicks prove, we evidently enjoy gossip very much.

It would, for example, have been very hard not to read at length in the Chinese media about the actor Wang Baoqiang and his wife Ma Rong. After a heady romance and years of apparent marital idyll, things fell apart for the couple when Ma Rong had an affair with Wang's manager Song Zhe. For weeks, Chinese media reported on Wang Baoqiang's rage and sense of betrayal, Ma Rong's dissatisfactions with her often absent husband, Song Zhe's attempts to justify his behaviour, and elite

Beijing's surprise and condemnation. To read such stories is obviously demeaning and idiotic—but plainly irresistible. If there is any way out of the conundrum, it is offered to us via the peculiar recognition that most of what we call great literature is in the end not so very far from gossip. Tolstoy's *Anna Karenina* could be described as little other than 800 pages of quasi gossip about an apparently idyllic couple, Anna and Count Karenin, torn apart by the former's affair with Vronsky, a cavalry officer, much to the surprise and condemnation of St Petersburg society.

But if in the end we resist calling Tolstoy a gossip, it has nothing to do with the topics he considers. It is entirely possible to talk a lot about someone's intimate existence, to take an interest in the details of their divorce, to wonder about their career or to reflect on their disgrace—and still not to be guilty of gossiping in any way. The activity is not defined by a particular subject matter, solely by the manner in which it is being considered. The *China Daily* or the *Sankt-Peterburgskie Vedomosti* could easily have turned the bare facts of Anna Karenina and Vronsky's affair into gossip, just as Tolstoy could have transformed news of Wang Baoqiang and Ma Rong's breakup into a masterful slice of Sino-Russian literature.

What identifies gossip is the pretence that only certain people are foolish, sexual, embarrassing and prone to lose their tempers or say things they regret. The gossiper holds unfortunate specimens in their tweezers, turns them over with glee and refuses to see any connection between every new shamed or ruined personality and their own flawed nature. They withhold the truth, on which every act of compassion is based, that we are all sinners, every last one of us, not merely this or that miserable creature unlucky enough to have attracted the malicious attention of the hard-hearted journalist.

We don't need to be great writers to avoid treating the intimate difficulties of others as gossip. We just need to keep seven important ideas in mind as we ruminate on the travails of people in the news: that insofar as they hurt anyone, they are extremely unlikely to have set out to do so; that the difficulties they caused are almost certainly unwitting by-products of passing weakness and idiocy; that they are liable to be mortified by what has happened and to long to make amends; that despite their possibly prestigious position or fortune, they were once a child, and, like all of us, are desperate to be held, treated with consideration and forgiven; that if you knew them properly, you would like them; that if you saw them sleeping, you couldn't hate them—and that if you dared to look at them adequately, you would recognise a version of yourself.

We can of course, and in terms of our psychological development probably should, spend time discussing the turmoils in the lives of influential people. Their difficulties present us with a chance to reflect on the powers of fate and the entanglements of the heart; we need to remember our humanity and our vulnerability as we do so. The difference between gossip and literature is love.

School was likely to have been—for most of us reading this—a deeply awful experience. The difficulty wasn't so much the homework, the boredom of lessons and the discipline of the teachers, however arduous these may have been. The difficulty would more likely have stemmed from having to live for most of the day within a totalitarian hierarchical value system—policed by a pitiless mob.

Depending on the school, what mattered above all would have been to be fashionable, thin, beautiful, sporty or strong. Anything else would have quickly marked us out for sabotage and destruction. If we preferred to read poetry, to lie on the carpet drawing flowers, to sing songs by Schubert, to pick our spots, to bake banana cake or to talk in a beguiling childlike way to our teddies, our fates would have been sealed. If we ever made a mistake (kissed the wrong person, made an unwise revelation to a jealous friend), there would have been no possibility of being forgiven: our classmates would have remembered everything until the day we left, and walking into the cafeteria at lunchtime would have been a trauma on every new occasion.

The one redeeming feature of school is that it had an endpoint in sight. However bad the bullying got, however cruel the nicknames, however many things were thrown our way as we searched for a place to sit at lunch, we knew that one day—eventually—it would be over. We would be able to leave and regain freedom, independence and dignity. Out in the wide-open spaces of the world, no one would need to know what we liked to do in our room, no one would be able to comment on what we were wearing, it wouldn't be anyone's business who we were dating, we would be able to get away from people who didn't like what we were listening to or what

Paparazzi waiting outside the
home of Amy Winehouse, 2009.

The comments below many
articles can quickly start to
resemble school toilets.

we esteemed, no one would remember what we did five years ago or why we had once acquired an enemy, there wouldn't be any more prefects or tormenters.

But one of the problems of the media lies in its power to recreate some of the atmosphere of school. The comments below many articles can quickly start to resemble those school toilets, confessionals of hate smelling of urine and bleach that would once have daily kept us informed of who had slept with whom, whose mother was a slag, and who needed to be killed.

Though we may be deep into adulthood, we may still need to take on board that—for the sake of our imprisoned psyches—our greatest priority is finally and urgently to leave school. We gave school the better part of our first two decades; we do not need to give our entire lives over to any of its successors in the mediatised world.

For most of history, however disappointed you might have been with people close to home, with your own hurtful family or maddening colleagues, you were at least able to hold on to a broader faith to tide you over the moments of despair: you could keep believing in humanity as a whole, in human beings in general, as opposed to this or that flawed, irritating or nasty local example. You could look over a large crowd celebrating a national event and—without knowing any of them in detail—could feel a warm and broad assurance that among these cheering neatly turned out people, there were sure to be plenty of sincere and kindly souls. You could be certain that for all of your frustrations and let-downs, you dwelt among fundamentally decent types, that even if you were very angry with your mother or full of resentment against the foreman, there was solace to be found in your nation and its peoples.

Yet patriotism and a benevolent sense of community are ultimately based on the privilege of not knowing too many of our fellow citizens very well. The closer we come to understanding anyone's real nature, the greater the risks of disappointment. Our own family and work colleagues aren't exceptionally awful; we simply know them uncommonly well.

Unfortunately for our powers of endurance, modern technology has done us one incalculable disservice: it has introduced us to one another on a global scale. There are no 'strangers' any longer, there are simply billions of people one can peer in on via their social media accounts and who are ready to introduce us to their ideas, their puppies, their relatives—and, along the way, their prejudices, their blind spots, their conspiracy theories, and their dispiriting enthusiasms for rage and cruelty.

Crowds outside Buckingham Palace
for the royal wedding, 1947.

It is the particular curse of our times that we can read
the diaries and streams of consciousness of everyone
on the planet. We can see them lining up to punch
anyone who is down; displaying obtuseness around
views they don't agree with; painting their ideological
enemies in unforgiving colours; caricaturing, envying
and resenting; acting sanctimoniously around every
transgression; behaving as if they were flawless;
leaving us certain that if ever we needed help or
sympathy, we wouldn't get it.

But there is hope here too. People aren't necessarily
cruel to begin with and they aren't inevitably committed to remaining so. They are—more than anything
—malleable; and they have been schooled in the very
wrong ways. Yet they could one day take inspiration
from other, better sources were these to be offered to
them. There might eventually be as much kindness
at large as there is currently viciousness or lack of
empathy, were the role models and public messages
to alter.

Distraction

1 —— Self-knowledge

A lot of the reason why we get mentally ill and unhappy is that there is so much about our lives that we fail to investigate and understand with honesty and courage. There's something wrong in our relationship, but we can't pin down what exactly and so go in for sarcasm and bitterness; we are beset by anxiety but we can't trace the pain back to any specific factors; we are irritable but we don't know what has made us furious deep down. We are in no doubt that there's something we should be doing to improve our career and make better use of our talents, but we never succeed in reaching a clear sense of our priorities or in charting a more plausible course.

We dwell instead in a miasma of self-ignorance, full of vague forebodings, unformed regrets and undiagnosed alarms. There is a fog between our conscious minds and our true selves. The vital truths dwell like pine trees in a heavy mist, as in Hasegawa Tohaku's screen (overleaf), struggling to break loose from an enveloping fog that envelops and conceals, teasing with their presence without ever becoming distinct.

We fail to investigate ourselves properly largely because doing so threatens to hurt a lot. We are, in the short term, profoundly invested in looking away; we are built so that whenever we come near to important realisations, we are visited by waves of anxiety and discomfort; we're inherently squeamish about working

Hasegawa Tohaku, *Pine Trees*
(Left-hand screen), 16th century.

out what is really going on inside. Knowledge threatens to upset the comfortable status quo: perhaps—after we reflect—we'll realise that we really have no option but to leave our present partner. We might have to confront just how unsatisfying our current career is; we might be furious with someone we are meant to love.

To ensure that we will never come face to face with ourselves, we develop addictions. We are used to categorising addictions chiefly in reference to drugs or alcohol. But this lets many of us off too lightly. Addiction isn't limited to a dependence on a chemical. An addiction is simply anything that guarantees that we will never have to come to terms with ourselves, that promises to ward off uncomfortable or dreadful inner realisations. Conceived of like this, a host of other types of addiction come into view: we might get addicted to doing exercise, reading football scores, worrying about insurance or going to work. An addiction can't be spotted by what it makes us do, simply by what it prevents us from feeling.

In this context, the media presents itself as the most tempting of all contemporary addictions. It is omnipresent, it understands our minds perfectly, it knows just how to tease and beguile us; above all, it is prestigious. It sounds so reasonable to say that we have been following the news; we couldn't possibly be declared mentally unwell merely for taking a profound interest in developments in the South China Sea or in the European Parliament.

But the ongoing swirl of news is the ideal instrument for destroying our strength to follow information from inside our minds. We deploy our curiosity about strangers to stifle any danger of decoding ourselves. It isn't that the news is inherently invaluable; someone should know about the exploding oil rig, the dissent in government, the affair in Malibu and the drop in the currency—but this shouldn't, right now, be us. We have priorities that aren't those set by the global media. The headlines to which we should be paying attention have to do with our emotional education and maturation. There are—strangely but truly—far more important stories to pay attention to than the most significant stories in the world.

Spending a few quiet hours staring out of the window isn't an activity with high prestige. Our busy, media-saturated age wants us to take action; there is always something new we should be reading, acquiring, fearing or longing for. It would be embarrassing to have to admit that, today, we did little other than stand close to the glass and take in the traffic, the wind in the trees, the muffled murmurs of pedestrians, the honking of cars and the flashing of advertising signs. We might not have checked the news since early morning.

Henri Matisse saw things differently. Throughout his career, he painted dozens of people staring out of windows—and tried to endow the pastime with new significance. In Nice in the early 1920s, he completed a series of works that featured a pensive, thoughtful-looking dancer and musician, Henriette Darricarrère. In one example, she looks out towards the Promenade des Anglais and the Baie des Anges, but the interest of the picture stems not so much from what she is seeing as from what we intimate she is feeling as she does so: there might be the slow unpacking of thoughts about an argument she had or about a difficult message she needed to impart. It's the inner view that is being fore-grounded and that calls out for our attention.

The point of window-gazing isn't to see outside, it's to give ourselves a better chance of perceiving what dwells in the unconscious beneath the daily chatter; it's our chance to make up for all the emotions we've been so careful not to entertain for too long and that have made us anxious and sad through inattention. The view is a tool to encourage some of our most salient and necessary ideas to make themselves known to us at last. We might learn more from a stretch of day-dreaming than from all the headlines in the world.

————

Henri Matisse, *Girl
by a Window*, 1921.

Debris in the aftermath of
Hurricane Michael in Mexico
Beach, Florida, 2018.

3 —— Memento mori

All our lives, under the influence of the media, we employ fears from without to distract us from fears from within. We worry about lightning storms, inflation, flying insects, contaminated spinach and UFOs—because it is, ultimately, easier to do so.

We have legitimate cause to worry a lot, but not about the president or the legislation, the asteroid or the arriving aliens. We have to worry that we have so little time left in order to sort out our relationships, that we still haven't determined how to love another human, that we don't properly know what fulfils us and that we aren't leading the authentic, courageous lives we are capable of.

This is the true horror; this is the spectre we need to see blinking on our phones on an hourly, even a minute-by-minute basis. It shouldn't matter to us that there was a typhoon off a distant coast last night. Those poor fishermen will have to take care of themselves and our sentimental concern won't appease their families for an instant. It isn't our business that a little girl has gone missing in a neighbouring country, that a movie star may now be seeing their personal trainer and that next year's watermelon crop may have been obliterated by a new kind of worm.

Our responsibility lies elsewhere entirely, with our own neglected genius, our perpetually stymied relationships and our unexamined childhood sorrows. We should be very scared—just seldom of what we're being actively told to worry about.

Part II

Media Cures

1 ———————————————————————————————

This Is Not the Whole World

The cure begins with a brutal proposal: there is no need for us to continue to understand the world through the media. Though almost everyone we come across will have been mesmerised by the same five or six stories, we do not need to join in. Our impression of 'what is going on' doesn't have to be decided on in a newsroom. We can become wilfully ignorant of what we're meant to know—in order to focus on our own wayward and preciously odd perceptions.

We will be able to congratulate ourselves on our liberation the day when we won't, against all odds, have heard anything about a film everyone has apparently seen, when we'll have forgotten almost every member of the cabinet, when a new technology company will mean nothing to us and when we can shrug our shoulders at news of a fresh scandal. We might—with sufficient discipline—even reach a stage where we can be shown one of the most famous pop stars in the world —and have no idea who it is.

??

Utagawa Hiroshige, *Night Rain In Karasak*, c. 1834.

We might proudly use our freedom to stock our minds with less familiar and more restorative nutrients. We might get curious about the panpipe music of the Solomon Islands, and the career of Edwin Nanau Sitori, who wrote 'Walkabout long Chinatown', the most revered song in the South Pacific. We'll be able to get interested in the woodcut images of rain by Utagawa Hiroshige and the peaceful renderings of ships at anchor at dawn by Emanuel Larsen. We'll be able to read novels by Gabriela Mistral and get around to the poetry of Saadi Shirazi. We'll watch films by Sevda Shishmanova and explore the architecture of Huỳnh Tấn Phát. We'll become secret exiles in our own societies; we'll be free.

To console us for the depredations and meanness of the world, we might at the same time reflect on and take solace from planets less noisy and contentious than our own. We could liberate ourselves from the status game and the rumours, the competitiveness and the moralism by regularly turning our thoughts to Mars, and the silent, windblown vistas of the Aeolis Palus plain near the equatorial Gale Crater, as captured by NASA's intrepid robots—to the indifference of almost our entire species.

The Twin Peaks, southwest of the
Mars Pathfinder landing site, 1999.

The Canberra Deep Space
Communication Complex,
Canberra, Australia.

We might think about the antennae belonging to the Deep Space Network in Canberra, Australia, that relay messages to the Voyager 2 probe, currently speeding through interstellar space at 15,341 km/s, or if we were yet wiser and more imaginative, we might think about the cows that habitually graze near these vast steel structures, caring not at all for the measurement of the density of interstellar plasma, let alone for the world's singers, politicians or prisoners, thinking only of the next mouthful of bluegrass, positioning themselves to catch the best of the sun, not getting agitated or em-bittered, not worrying what might be said about them, not caring how they could appear to others. How much we might understand if we didn't learn what everyone else knows.

We would, in our more wisely ignorant state, be able to keep our thoughts moving in optimally enriching grooves. Rather than being tossed into random mania or lust with every check of our feeds, we would irrigate our minds with only the calmest, most steadying, least agitating reflections. We could keep fragments of anci-ent literature and religion in mind, we would remember nursery rhymes, we would echo the ideas of sages, we would learn poems off by heart. We would not ruin every promising day by turning immediately to that small glowing instrument of control and unhappiness waiting for us by the bed.

You Can Look Elsewhere

There have always been people who learnt to disconnect and look elsewhere. One of the most determined and inspiring was the Abbot Armand de Rancé. Born in Paris in 1626 into a noble and prominent family, he squandered his youth in frivolity and vanity: he had lovers, he got into fights, he drank too much, he boasted of his status, he dabbled in politics and he fought some duels. Then, at the age of 34, he suffered a spiritual crisis, or what we would now term a breakdown: he could no longer bear the superficiality of his friends, the petty intrigues of Parisian life, the noise and chatter of the salons and the great houses and the sinfulness of politics.

Hyacinthe Rigaud, *Armand Bouthillier Rancé*, c. 1743.

So, to the surprise of his acquaintances (he had been one of the richest and most eligible men in Europe), he gave away all his possessions, took a vow of celibacy, pledged himself to God and went to live in the isolated Abbey of La Trappe in a quiet valley two days to the east of Paris. There, he instituted a range of austere reforms that emphasised silence, retreat from the world and solitary contemplation—the hallmarks of a new Catholic order that came to be known, in honour of the newly revived monastery, as the Trappists. A key part of de Rancé's mission was to shut out the world from his monks' lives so that they could better concentrate on the divinity and omnipotence of the creator. He knew how much anything—a letter, an appointment, a gathering—could spoil a day. So he banned all visitors, he had the walls extended and raised, and he persuaded Louis XIV to remove a highway that ran outside the monastery's front gate—so that not even the sound of hooves would disturb the peace. De Rancé was reputed not to have said anything for two years.

The 19th-century writer Chateaubriand, who considered de Rancé one of the greatest figures in French history, added that he was also the person with the most to teach the noisy, chattering modern age, a rapidly industrialising technological world in which silence and inner poise had been eradicated. Like his hero, Chateaubriand had begun with a noisy life: he had been an intimate of Napoleon, a friend of statesmen, the French Ambassador to London, an acclaimed chronicler and a well-known politician in post-Restoration France. But he grew tired of intrigue, gossip, slander, rumours and the corrupt and mediocre nature of most human beings. He longed for silence and focus. Though he could not summon the faith required to live in an actual monastery, inspired by de Rancé, he decided to live as a quasi-secular Trappist in his own home. For the last fifteen years of his life, he holed himself up in his apartment at 120 rue du Bac in Paris—and never went

Grave of Chateaubriand,
Grand Bé, France.

FIRST SERIES—(*continued.*)

Media Cures

25

26

27

28

29

30

A.M. Worthington, *A Study of Splashes*, 1908.

out. There were no more parties, debates, lecture tours, seductions or dinners. He proposed that only an imbecile would fail to want to be famous when young, and only a fool would want to be anything other than a hermit when old. His last book was a short, brilliant biography of de Rancé, which he hoped would remind posterity of the silent abbot's achievements. Committed to reclusiveness, the elderly Chateaubriand left precise instructions that when he died he should be buried on the remote windswept island of Grand Bé near Saint-Malo—which can only be reached with some difficulty at low tide.

Monasticism has not been much in vogue for a century and a half at least, but the hunger that animated the movement lives on in modern humans, and perhaps beats with a greater intensity than it has ever done. We lack a guiding ideology around which a truly disciplined isolated life could be built, but many of us remain highly susceptible to, and moved by, the call of bare limestone walls, serene ecclesiastical spaces, empty days spent in reflection—and the opportunity to block out the many distractions that prevent us from understanding our past and making peace with ourselves.

There are nevertheless plenty of ways in which we can take inspiration from the seclusion of monk-like figures to bring greater harmony to our minds—and could find no end of substitutes for the majesty of God to focus our thoughts on. One example of a secular contemplative spirit was the English scientist Arthur Worthington, who, in the late 19th century, cut himself off from society in order to study—with some of the reverence and single-minded commitment of a religious devotee —the dynamics of water droplets as they hit dry earth or a puddle. In two landmark works, *The Splash of a Drop* (1895) and *A Study of Splashes* (1908), Worthington minutely analysed the distortions and velocities of water on a variety of downward trajectories. There were chapters on the characteristic size of droplets, their differing propensities to give birth to satellite beads of water and the variety of sounds that these made on impact. To help his audiences better understand the science, Worthington photographed over a hundred drops in various states—gifting the world both an extraordinary homage to the subtlety of nature and one of the most moving testimonies of what focused reclusive ego-less thought can produce.

Andy Warhol might have had a reputation for attending a great many parties and maintaining a hypnotic interest in the news, but he always remained a devoted Catholic and experienced regular powerful longings to retreat, rediscover silence and focus on the hidden grace of the ordinary world. A lot of his work can be read as ambivalent dialogue with the mass media, both admiring its glamour and drama and despising it for pulling us away from sincerity and modest truths. In 1964, in a wry protest at the proliferation of fast-moving images and urgent dispatches, Warhol directed a film titled *Empire*. It was first shown to a keenly excited crowd on the 6th of March 1965 at the City Hall Cinema in Manhattan. What the crowd had not expected was that the film would be eight hours long and that nothing at all would happen in it. Unlike any work in the history of American cinema, the film had no characters, no drama, no progression and no denouement. All there was was a camera that had been perfectly trained on the Empire State Building from a few blocks away and that had recorded everything that happened to this landmark over a period of time. After a few hours, viewers were invited to note a flight of pigeons across the screen. A few times some seagulls made an appearance. There was the odd plane in the sky. Once, what might have been a moth inched across the lens. And, in perhaps the most dramatic event in the film, there was a changing of patterns of lights inside the skyscraper itself as people left their offices to go home at the end

Six and a half hours into *Empire*
by Andy Warhol, 1964.

of the day. It was as if God, or a Trappist monk, had been looking out of the window in midtown. But none of this passionate, devoted observation satisfied the audience. Frustrated by the lack of action, they suspected that they were the victims of an elaborate joke, and halfway through the film a riot broke out, many of the seats were ripped up and thrown across the auditorium and security had to be called. Warhol left in fear and disgust.

Useful Pessimism

Some of the reason why the media is so easily able to rile, mesmerise, scare and infuriate us comes from a counter-intuitive thesis: because we are too hopeful. Though we may not think of ourselves as optimists, in a range of areas we unwittingly adopt a recklessly expectant and idealistic philosophy—which leaves us open to continuous jolts of disappointment and alarm.

Despite a lot of evidence to the contrary, we continue to insist on believing that governments will be competent, that large changes to the way nations are run can occur within days, that planes don't get delayed, that people don't kill one another, that there aren't any thieves or hijackers, that hospitals never get too full, that companies are never mismanaged and that apparently contented people don't sometimes jump off bridges.

With such buoyant views in mind, it is no achievement on the part of the media to be able to shock and anger us every day with the dramas it uncovers. And yet how much less troubled we would be if we could only accept from the outset that we were living in a fallen world, in which—tragically but unavoidably—appalling things were certain to unfold at pretty much every hour.

When confronting yet another bit of terrible news, we might learn something from the biblical prophet Jeremiah. According to the Old Testament, Jeremiah was born in a village north of Jerusalem around 650 BCE. When he was in his mid-twenties, he had a visit from God, who told him in grave terms that the

Jewish people would suffer a succession of disasters in the years ahead due to their lack of morality and obedience. They would be visited by famine, war and disease, and their capital Jerusalem would be razed to the ground and all its inhabitants taken into captivity. Even worse, there was nothing the people of Judah could do to prevent this; Jeremiah's mission was simply to tell them what was on the cards, not to offer hope or alternatives. Sure enough, in 586 BCE, the Babylonians under the command of Nebuchadnezzar II laid siege to Jerusalem, annihilated the defenders, burnt down the sacred Solomon's Temple and took the population off to be slaves in Babylon. Jeremiah didn't—as he might have done—start screaming; he didn't pound his fist, implore God or accuse anyone of betrayal. He just sat very quietly reflecting on a terribleness that he had always anticipated and then wrote a short work known to us as the Book of Lamentations—that emphasises the sinfulness and preordained agony of existence.

In 1630, Rembrandt—no stranger to misfortune himself —opted to depict Jeremiah just after he had heard the news of Jerusalem's destruction. He sits with one elbow on the Bible, slumped and sad, with the embers of the once famed city glowing in the background. Crucially, he isn't shouting and he isn't protesting. He had known for years that this was going to happen, and it had. It did not make it any less awful, but it did make it, importantly, less surprising. There was no need, on top of everything else, for Jeremiah to be incensed. He had never been promised ease and sure enough was never going to taste it. It was this resigned pessimism that so appealed to Rembrandt, who turned Jeremiah into a hero of grief, a role model for how we might ourselves approach our sorrows and those of our nations. The headlines might seek to make us scream; we would be wiser simply to take note and then briefly mutter 'but of course.'

Rembrandt van Rijn, *Jeremiah
Lamenting the Destruction
of Jerusalem*, 1630.

Josse Lieferinxe, *Saint Sebastian Interceding for the Plague Stricken*, 1497–1499.

Yet pessimism should not depress us. Indeed, knowing how often there have been problems and yet how —despite everything—civilisation proceeds should lend us a measure of tart comfort for the dark stretches we will have to go through. Far more than the media ever lets us know, we can take agony—and rebuild and recover. When the next calamity strikes, we should think that we have been here before, so many times before. For example:

——— When, in the 27th century BCE, the Nile failed to flood for seven successive years and caused one of the first and largest famines in Egyptian history. Hieroglyphs record that the national calamity was resolved only when Pharaoh Djoser ordered the construction of a giant temple to appease the temperamental and vain Nile river god, Khnum: the waters rose again the following year.

——— We have been here before when, on 13th December CE 115, a devastating earthquake hit the ancient city of Antioch, destroying three quarters of its buildings and killing half of its 500,000 inhabitants in minutes. Reconstruction work continued for a decade.

——— We've been here before when a devastating tsunami shored at Alexandria on 21st July CE 365. 50,000 people were killed in the busy port city and its surroundings. The city's Royal Quarter disappeared permanently underwater, only to be rediscovered by a chance dig for a cable in 1995.

——— We've been here before when the first global bubonic plague pandemic began raging in Constantinople in CE 542, having entered via the busy trade routes from Asia. Known as the plague of Justinian, it continued to infect the Mediterranean world for another 225 years, disappearing only in CE 750 after killing some 50 million people.

———— We've been here before when, in 1346, the 'Black Death' arrived in Europe from the Russian steppes and killed a quarter of the continent's population—an estimated 25 million people.

———— We've been here before when in 1519 Hernán Cortés landed on the shores of what is now Mexico and what was then the Aztec Empire bringing in his saliva the smallpox virus, which in the next hundred years killed ninety-five per cent of the population of Central and South America.

———— We've been here before when, on 23rd January 1556, one of the deadliest earthquakes ever recorded in history occurred in the densely populated province of Shaanxi, China. Building collapses and mudslides killed an estimated 830,000 people.

———— We've been here before when, on 1st November 1755, an earthquake shattered Lisbon and drove the surviving population to the shoreline, where they were met by a gigantic tsunami. The combination made off with 30,000 people and at a stroke ended the optimism of the European Enlightenment.

———— We've been here before when the largest volcanic eruption in human history occurred at Mount Tambora, Indonesia, in April 1815, killing 71,000 people and creating an ash cloud that reduced global temperatures by 0.4 degrees Celcius, leading to major food shortages, epidemics and civil unrest around the world for the following three years.

———— We've been here before when monsoon failures in 1837 and 1838 led to famine in the north-western Indian provinces of Punjab and Rajasthan, killing 800,000 people. The economic and social disruption, and the cholera that came with it, live on in Indian memory to this day.

———— We've been here before when a third global bubonic plague pandemic broke out in 1894. The crisis lasted on and off for twenty years, its global spread accelerated by steam travel and the scale of imperial trade networks. Worldwide, 15 million died; India was by far the worst hit, with 10 million deaths.

———— We've been here before when, in 1896–1898, over ninety-five per cent of Southern Africa's cattle herds were wiped out by a devastating panzootic of rinderpest. Coinciding with a severe drought and crop failures, this resulted in unprecedented famine in the Northern Transvaal. Desperate, people ate roots, caterpillars and old animal hides; many resorted to drowning their children.

———— We've been here before when, in 1918–1919, the influenza pandemic known as the 'Spanish Flu' killed over 50 million people, far eclipsing the deaths of the First World War, a mere 20 million.

We have been in grave trouble before—and we will be so again. But, as the media are careful never to tell us, we will endure.

After thirty-seven years in captivity, the Jews of Babylon were eventually released by the emperor Cyrus the Great—and returned to Judah. The temple was rebuilt. And then, a few generations later, new trouble having brewed, it was destroyed again. Of course.

The Clothes of Our Era

It can be tempting to think of ourselves as individuals, as people who make their own choices utterly free of any influence from others, who obey only their hearts, who refuse to subscribe to groupthink and who carve their particular and distinctive paths through the monolithic assumptions of mass society. That is, it is easy to think like this until we see a photograph of any random group of people in a large city in an era other than our own.

Young women in Carnaby Street, London, 1968.

The young women advancing together in the sunshine along Carnaby Street in London's West End in 1968 were, at the time, entirely certain of their individuality. In their eyes, they were icons of modern freedom. They weren't anything like their conformist mothers or grand-mothers, pious aunts or timid school friends. They had thrown off the shackles of tradition; they had stopped worrying about being respectable; they no longer cared what other people were thinking. They were simply—at last—able to be whoever they wanted.

But what immediately strikes us in retrospect is how extraordinarily submissive they were to the rules of their own highly identifiable era. The look they had adopted—straight mid-length hair, short dresses, bold, plain colours, an absence of conspicuous jewellery— was not something that they had invented or selected for themselves. They were just closely following the style guidelines laid out that year by an energetic fashion designer called Mary Quant, whose nearby shop —Bazaar—had been seized on by the media as the epicentre of contemporary fashion. Their imagined freedom was a symptom of an underlying determination to stick as closely as possible to a media-generated vision of style.

The media didn't limit itself to hemlines and hairstyles. It was essential (as Mary Quant emphasised) to have 'optimistic and vibrant' personalities. She didn't have to add—because the meaning was plain—that being melancholy, nostalgic or solemn was no longer a good idea. This was no longer a time for the poetry of Rudyard Kipling, a reverence for the British Empire or an enthu-siasm for Elgar. It was necessary to like abstract art, concrete architecture and pop music. Should a fash-ionable person discover in themselves a burgeoning attraction to Gothic cathedrals, Dutch still life or military brass brands, they would have needed to remain very silent.

Members of the Ziegfeld Follies visiting the
Arc de Triomphe du Carrousel, Paris, 1924.

None of this hidden deference was the fault of the young women themselves. In following the fashion of the day, they were simply doing what most of us have done since the genesis of structured society; namely, stick very closely—in both outward form and inner conviction—to the dominant story of what we are supposed to be like. It is only a special vanity that makes us miss what we are up to.

No doubt the women standing in front of the Arc de Triomphe du Carrousel in Paris in 1924 also thought of themselves as rather authentic. Unlike their mothers and aunts, they had—by themselves, apparently—decided to wear cloche hats, long fur coats and strings of pearls. They favoured jazz music, cycling holidays, Cubist art and poetry about fallen heroes. They were convinced of their freedom—but they were naturally only meekly following the bugle call of their own mass media.

Real freedom isn't to be found in adopting a script but in probing possibilities that extend far beyond those recognised as plausible by the media at any given point. The styles, fashions, interests and enthusiasms that are so strongly endorsed cannot possibly cover the full range of our inclinations. We are born naked, with no particular predetermination to wear miniskirts rather than swirling robes or let our hair hang loose rather than cover our heads with wide-brimmed hats or beanies. We should take a long time to consider who we might really be—and what might suit us.

We might, after deliberation, then become one of those rare and unusual figures who on a Friday evening slips out of their contemporary work clothes and, for a few days, don what feels like more appropriate and personally targeted kinds of leisure wear. We might —as enthusiasts of historical re-enactments—dress up as Roman centurions or medieval knights, American Indians or 18th-century European aristocrats; we might take part in mock battles and jousting tournaments, do a foxtrot or a waltz in an uncommonly grand ballroom, declaim some lines by Homer or sing songs by Gilbert and Sullivan—and feel ourselves to be true to our spirit at last.

It is seldom that anyone ever really becomes who they are so long as they are still widely regarded as normal by others. We'll probably accede to our true individuality, and break free from the ideology of our age, only when a sizeable number of people start to think of us as weird—or, under their breath, simply mad.

Members of an amateur historical
re-enactment society recreate the
Battle of Agincourt, England, 2018.

Become an Aristocrat

One way to try to survive a media-dominated world would be to do your best to become an aristocrat.

Aristocrats are, of course, a faintly ridiculous proposition: they wear tweed clothes; they speak with improbable accents; they have odd-sounding (often very long) names; they bury themselves in the depths of the country on estates that have been in their families for generations, devoting themselves to the slaughter of foxes and grouse; they are low on talent and ill-equipped for competition in a meritocratic society.

But they have one very enviable merit: they are utterly indifferent to popular opinion. It never occurs to them that what they care about could get a fair hearing in the media. They accept that they belong to a radical minority and that it would be absurd to imagine that the average person would know about, let alone be sympathetic to, their world. This gives them the strength to approach the media with light-hearted indifference. They don't blame or even dislike the popular press for not understanding them: it is entirely inevitable. The vast majority of the population are—in their eyes—simply unfortunate people who at some level mean well but can't conceivably have opinions worth taking too seriously. Aristocrats are not politically antidemocratic, they are something quite different and more intriguing: they are psychologically above popular opinion.

We might rather wish we could share some of their unconcern, but how can we—who lack castles and long lines of fancy ancestors—possibly have access to this elevated and blithe state of mind?

The dilemma received one intriguing answer in France in the 19th century. Traditionally, aristocrats had been defined by their huge economic and political power. But in the Revolution of 1789, many of them lost their heads and even more lost their money, so a new definition started to be explored. A pivotal figure in this was the novelist and essayist Jules Barbey d'Aurevilly. Born in 1808 into the Normandy gentry, his family had for generations been allied with the grand lords who ruled the nation. Yet now they had lost their lands and their homes—but they still wished to signal that they were not like everyone else. Barbey d'Aurevilly tried to give a form to a sense of superiority that did not depend on lineage or money: he might no longer have been at the top of society in sheer material terms but he possessed—so he thought—a different and more important title. He was one of the initiators of a new idea of an aristocracy: an aristocracy of the Spirit, rather than of the Blood. To be an aristocrat in the modern world—he suggested—was a matter of possessing elegant taste, sensibility, lofty ideas and refined emotions. This, rather than the possession of large tracts of land and a chateau or two, was what gave one the keys to the elite.

In his own life, Barbey d'Aurevilly expressed his attitude by adopting an extravagant mode of dress and self-presentation. He was fond of lace cuffs and he often wore an elaborate cravat; he grew a vast moustache, adopted a haughty posture and perfected a way of lifting his chin, lowering his eyelids and gazing down his nose to convey a profound lack of concern for what people in general might think of him, or—indeed—of anything else. It wasn't his bloodline that he thought set him apart, it was his soul. He resolutely opposed the notion of popularity. The ideal, he said, was 'to be

Émile Lévy, *Jules Barbey d'Aurevilly*, 1882.

a genius and to be obscure' (although he was, in fact, rather widely read in his own times). Loftiness and intensity of mind did not need popular endorsement.

Barbey d'Aurevilly was putting a finger on a crucial possibility: that there might be a modern, workable version of a legitimate aristocratic disdain for public opinion. It could be reasonable to see yourself as being 'above' the populist debate, without possessing an estate or an ancient name, just because you had a different sort of mind.

Sadly, Barbey d'Aurevilly was too emotionally attached to the vision of *looking* special to fully articulate the deeper implication of his thought. In reality, a pure Aristocrat of the Spirit could look entirely normal, live in a perfectly ordinary house and have a common enough job and never sport a cravat. None of the dandyish garb of 19th-century Aristocrats of the Spirit was really necessary. What should in essence set Aristocrats of the Spirit apart is a commitment to mental refinement.

Their disdain for popular opinion isn't the result of ill will or hostility; it arises from a sober and careful analysis of the human condition. Most people just are not interested in understanding an opposing opinion; blind partisanship is simply far more tempting. It may be unfortunate that almost no one has a taste for unpicking the exact logic of an argument—but nothing in history should lead us to expect that they would. It's surely a pity that millions are more eager to denounce than to explain, but it's hardly surprising. A love of accurate explanation is almost as rare as the ownership of a castle.

The pure Aristocrat of the Spirit ignores public opinion not because they hate people but because they know them well and are sympathetic and compassionate towards the reasons why they won't be thinking straight. They feel an immense tenderness towards the ordinary preoccupations and struggles of daily life that mean that intricate argumentation, tenderness, open-mindedness and the delicate weighing of possibilities are unreachable luxuries for most. They are set apart not by haughty contempt but by a melancholic certainty that the disputes of the populace will be chaotic, brutal, partisan, deeply illogical and unfair because this is the normal, unfortunate lot of the human animal. These aristocrats don't take any of it to heart. They never hoped to be widely understood or popularly appreciated.

Just as the Aristocrat of the Blood once did, the new Aristocrat of the Spirit takes pride in their genealogy. But they are no longer talking about DNA. They belong to the great dynastic family of everyone who has shared their sensitivity, their suffering and their nobility of mind. They discover that Stendhal was an ancestor and Rembrandt was a member of their clan; Jane Austen perhaps was a relative or possibly Leo Tolstoy. They are—with great legitimacy—laying claim to a different but entirely real kind of nobility: one of ideas, responses, emotions, doubts, worries, pleasures, aspirations and complications, the common heritage of a small, but very lovely lineage. And so, they—we—can look on the disorders of democratic debate in the mass media without anxiety or distress. For we inhabit a very different kind of castle: one made of sensitivity rather than stone, just as enduring and open to all free-thinking newcomers—though invisible to the eyes of most.

Never Be Famous

Many people who are wary of fame may seek it out nevertheless because it can seem like the only way in which their talents can become known and their income assured. Fame isn't so much an end in itself as a necessary step to the life they want to lead.

The notion that fame might be a prerequisite of a successful career has a long history. One of its earliest proponents was a Renaissance Italian goldsmith and designer, Benvenuto Cellini. Born in Florence in 1500, Cellini began as a masterful but anonymous artisan. He specialised in small decorative articles for the home and the table; his salt cellars were especially impressive. But no one knew his name or cared particularly who he was or how his love life was structured (he was quietly dating two young men simultaneously, Domenico and Francesco, while also courting an aristocratic woman who had posed for one of his sculptures of a nymph). Then, at a certain point, Cellini discovered that if he foregrounded his complicated and boisterous person- ality, his work could attract a great deal more attention and fetch far higher prices. He therefore began assid- uously publishing stories of his daring adventures and radical opinions, he got his friends to boost his profile, he tipped off people about his romantic exploits, he had himself portrayed in dramatic postures and he wrote a wildly boastful, but very racy, autobiography.

As his fame grew, Cellini gained an ever-wider market for his work. He was perhaps the first designer to be collected across Europe simply on the basis of the prestige of his personal identity. Fashionable people aspired to own not just a beautiful and accomplished piece of tableware or sculpture, but—first and foremost—'a Cellini'.

Cellini's example changed sensibilities: it came to look as though personal publicity would always need to be a critical part of creative endeavour. Cellini presented his times and our own with a brittle choice: either one could be famous and effective or unknown and consigned to oblivion. A new kind of terror entered into the minds of ambitious but shy and undemonstrative people: that their lives would be wasted so long as their personalities remained hidden. How could one take oneself seriously as a potter, an artist, a playwright, a poet, an architect, a film director or indeed a designer of knives and forks unless one's name appeared on many people's lips?

The consequences of Cellini's initiative took a long time to become apparent, because it was only with the development of the modern media that fame really started to exert its full and dire toll. As late as the 19th century, it was still possible to be famous and yet remain in key ways untouched. In Britain, in the 1820s, even the prime minister Lord Liverpool was able to walk down London streets without any entourage and attract no notice or abuse.

Such quiet now seems inconceivable. The details of every famous person's life—their home address, their favourite holiday destinations, the strangeness of certain of their opinions, their marital ups and downs, their last love affair—all become public knowledge and the subject of incessant rumours and unkind speculations. Fame corrupts the most ordinary of moments: to sit in a restaurant invites strangers to approach them mid-mouthful to ask for a photograph; at the dry cleaners, they may be pointed at and asked to do more of the sort of work they finished doing ten years ago;

A 'Cellini' salt cellar,
c. 1540–1543.

Benvenuto Cellini, *Bearded Man*,
c. 1540–1543. A selfie of Cellini.

collecting the children at the school gates requires an array of evasive smiles; new friendships are beset by tangled preconceptions; new relationships immediately become the subject of envious judgements. And yet, even as the corrosive effects of fame have grown, Cellini's original proposition has survived. The talented continue to believe that being famous must be the only way to thrive; it is just that now their lives also happen to be substantially destroyed in the process.

Yet, we might ask, are Cellini's ideas truly valid and his conclusions inescapable? Is publicity always so necessary, let alone a sensible basis for deploying our abilities? Is there no way to escape the fateful choice between fame and creative fulfilment on the one hand and anonymity and desolation on the other?

One more hopeful approach is to be found in the case of a highly academically distinguished but (hopefully) still wholly unknown Russian mathematician, Grigori Perelman. On the basis of his significant achievements in the incomprehensibly technical fields of topology and Riemannian geometry, Perelman found himself—in the mid-2000s—on the cusp of global celebrity. He was offered a string of prestigious prizes, television programmes, newspaper interviews, sponsorship deals and party invitations, and these, together with his noble forehead, Romantic hair and wistful eyes, perfectly equipped him to be launched on the world stage as that stock figure of the modern popular imagination: the 'genius'. But instead of embracing the spotlight, Perelman decisively turned his back on every kind of attention. He declined prizes, he refused interviews, he avoided being photographed, he hired professionals to hide his tracks—and he made sure that, unless someone was directly interested in his extremely arcane field of work, they would never have a clue who he was. In a final public statement, he declared his firm intention never to become 'a creature in a zoo'.

Grigori Perelman, who (hopefully)
you will never have heard of.

Perelman's response might have appeared eccentric, but he established an extremely mature and unusually wily relationship to hyperintrusive media. He realised, as so few of the creative ever have the confidence or insight to do while there is still time, that whatever the short-term financial or social impact of being unknown, obscurity would save his life. He also saw that fame is not inevitable. It is possible to avoid its depredations —and still have a very interesting, albeit slightly more gradual and less dramatic, career. Whatever publicists and agents might claim, there is no need to give talks or appear on television. You can do well without ever bothering to give an interview to a Sunday newspaper. You do not need a social media profile. Whenever possible, you can submit work anonymously. You can adopt a pseudonym. You can even hide behind a coll-ective brand: *The Economist*—the world's foremost financial publication—subtly shields its writers from fame by never naming any of them. The magazine is well known but the individuals behind it have no bylines and retain all the grace of privacy; you might be sitting next to the editor and be none the wiser. Such an approach could be extended with ease to singers, psychotherapists or designers. There is no need to put your name on everything you do or make.

Such a discussion may seem to be relevant only to those few individuals who are looking to pursue a high-level creative career. But the implications are much broader. It is also we, the unfamous, who are the victims of the modern cult of fame, for societies that require us to be famous in order to acquire adequate attention and respect will necessarily only accord neglect and snobbish disregard to those who are unknown. An uncomfortable division will forever exist between day-to-day humiliation on the one hand and overexposure and intrusive renown on the other. The opposite of our dangerous cult of fame is not neglect but discernment. In a world without fame, certain books, sofas, cheeses or lamps will still be better than others, certain ideas will still be more valuable, certain people will still have hearts that are kinder and more sensitive, but none of these would have to be identified by the destructive and manic spotlight of the media. We, the general public, would be left to make up our own minds about where significance lay: what the good buildings were, what songs felt nicest to listen to, who we really most enjoyed spending time with. Talent and kindness would no longer have to court the reductive forces of pub-licity. Things would have a chance to be judged on their own merits, for their qualities, for their private allure and for their power to speak intimately to our souls. At the same time, no one would need to be photographed on their way back from a difficult first date or need to die young from the chilling consequences of being too widely known to many callous and intrusive strangers.

At the very time when Benvenuto Cellini was working in Italy and France, on the other side of the world, during what is known as Japan's Muromachi period, someone was putting their efforts to a series of bowls, water jars, tea caddies and serving dishes. Many were finished with an uneven bluey-brown glaze. They looked almost haphazard and yet at the same time entirely beguiling. They remain some of the finest pieces of ceramic ever made—and have consistently been of great interest to collectors and fetch enormous prices at auction. But fortunately, none of this has anything to do with who made them—for we have never and will never know. It might have been a man or a woman, a collective or a lone genius, someone who had three partners living in Edo and another (of another gender) married in Onomichi or someone who had taken a vow of celibacy after becoming a Zen priest at a monastery in Kamakura at 15; it matters not a jot. We have no clue and therefore are in an authentic position calmly to observe what is really in front of our eyes: a work of art whose beauty we can cherish as much as we do its—and our own —anonymity.

Japanese Tea Bowl with Hare's-Fur
Decoration, 16th century.

Think Like a Tragedian

A central ambition of the media has been to find monsters who can be held up to the public gaze as incarnations of evil and unite us in paroxysms of fury and disgust. We long to hear stories of the worst misdeeds in order to alleviate our sense of our own problematic natures; compared to strafing a school playground with a machine gun, detonating a bomb in a nightclub or keeping sex slaves chained in a basement, we appear almost innocent and even positively decent. In the 'monster stories' of the media, the most divided communities discover a convincing point of absolute agreement.

Towards the end of the 20th century, the American media came to focus its unbounded revulsion on a Californian woman, then in her early thirties, called Susan Eubanks. In October 1997—in the wake of fights with her estranged husband Eric and her new lover, Rene—Eubanks shot and killed her four sons: the eldest, Brandon, was 14; Matthew, the youngest, only 4. Rene, Eric and another three boyfriends before them had all cheated on Susan—and it had broken her mind. She left a note to Eric saying: 'you betrayed me ... I've lost everyone I've ever loved. Now it's time for you to do the same.' Then she turned the gun on herself. The bullet lodged in her abdomen, but she survived. She was put on trial, and after an unusually speedy deliberation, was sentenced to death.

The media were remorseless; all of Eubanks's inadequacies as a mother were charted in detail and her

Susan Eubanks, on trial for the
murder of her four sons, 1997.

claims that she had deeply loved her children were met
with derision and disgust. It was clear to every news
outlet that she was one of the most despicable people
who had ever lived.

And yet there remains a deep paradox within Susan
Eubanks's treatment because—unremarked upon by
any commentator—her story almost precisely mirrors
that of one of Western culture's most revered literary
heroines, Medea, who first appeared in a play of the
same name by Euripides, performed in Athens at the
festival of Dionysus in 431 BCE. The play follows Medea,
a princess living in the Greek city of Colchis, who has
befriended and fallen in love with the charismatic

heroic adventurer Jason. Medea helps Jason to steal the fabled Golden Fleece and, against the strongest opposition of her family and friends, marries him, moves to Corinth and has two sons with him. But after ten years of marriage, Jason abruptly informs Medea that the relationship is over and that he plans to marry a beautiful younger woman, Glauce, daughter of the king of Corinth. Humiliated and frantic, unable to think straight or contain herself, Medea punishes Jason in the most violent and definitive way she can conceive of: by putting their two children to death.

Despite the horror of what unfolds on stage, the play leaves us in no doubt that we are not meant to hate Medea in any straightforward way. No one would leave the theatre muttering 'monster'. It is Euripides' genius to present us with a highly disturbed and vengeful person who performs one of the worst deeds anyone is capable of while not allowing us to label her as evil. He shows us too much of her character and her motivations for caricature to be possible. We can see that she is agonised, desperate, driven to fury—but also loving, intelligent and deeply and profoundly miserable in a way that draws out our compassion. Euripides never suggests that murdering children might be excusable, but he leads us far into Medea's inner life to show us that she is still an unfortunate creature with whom we are able to empathise and at some level identify. She is a version of all of us, if we were to be pushed hard enough by events.

Yet the sad irony is that despite our respect for Medea as a character at large on a stage, our feelings for people like Medea in real life remain entirely untouched and untutored. In 1999, the year of Susan Eubanks's trial, over a dozen major performances of *Medea* were held across the United States, but they had no effect whatsoever on the tenor in which the betrayed and troubled child murderer was assessed. From the

San Jose *Mercury News* to the *New York Post*, it was unanimously agreed that Eubanks was an unfathomable monster who needed to be put to death by the US government as mercilessly and as swiftly as possible.

Few of us are in any danger of one day killing our children, but all of us are constantly guilty of a multitude of smaller but still grievous errors—in relation to which we tend to speak to ourselves and others as the tabloids addressed Eubanks rather than as Euripides handled Medea. If Euripides stands at one end of the spectrum of understanding, then the daily news—with its crude language of 'perverts' and 'weirdos' and its blindness to the universality of sin and error—stands at the other.

The point is not to try to become a great tragedian but to learn from art a tolerance and imaginative sympathy that we can come to practise on ourselves and on those who have transgressed around us. Art bids us to surrender viciousness and one-dimensionality in order to be gentler towards the follies of which we are, in different measures, all guilty. Euripides is the voice of an intimately and urgently needed benevolence.

None of us—even those among us who have done the very worst things—are ever 'monsters', deserving of the hatred of the entire world. We are just troubled, sad, frightened, lonely and immoderately desperate. We commit appalling deeds out of despair and damage, not innate badness; we need clinical assistance, not death row. More than two thousand years after Euripides, we are still waiting for a news service that could remotely honour his vision.

Eugène Delacroix, *Medea
about to Kill her Children*, 1838.

Know Who You Are

The media does not hold back from judgement. While ostensibly only reporting on events, it is constantly—and surreptitiously—handing down broader verdicts as to how we should live and what we should value. It tells us who is reputable and who is shameful, what a decent relationship is, how sexuality should be managed, what sums of money we need to make, who is a sinner, who is admirable, who is evil—and at times, if we are in the public eye, how we look, how worthwhile our work is and whether or not we deserve to be lauded.

There can be agony in encountering such judgements. Doing so can make us realise that the way we like to lead our relationships doesn't accord with what higher journalistic authorities have decreed to be 'normal'. We can be told that our desires and aspirations are perverted or reactionary. Our opinions may be categorised as damnable or odd. We may learn that our professional lives are not going a way the media deems impressive. Every now and then, we may find an article directly telling us that we should never bother to wake up.

None of this is ever going to be easy, but it may become a lot more so once we have managed to do something that, though it may sound pat or obvious, requires an uncommon and admirable degree of effort and mental strength to pull off: know ourselves better.

What we mean by knowing ourselves in this context is the process of developing an ample impression of the reasons why we hold certain views, why we are doing particular things and why our past is as it is. Once we have examined ourselves thoroughly, we won't necessarily approve of everything we are or have been, but we will understand how and why things came to be a certain way. Our relationship might be at odds with our times, but we'll grasp how—given our distinctive childhoods and the way our personalities were formed—it might make sense for us. We might not be completely proud of our income, but we'll see why our particular confluence of talents and inhibitions led us down a path that we can be reconciled to. And while we might not be proud of every word in a book we wrote or every frame in a film we made, we'll own what we have done, we'll know where the impulse to create as we did came from—we won't be seeking external validation, and nor will external condemnation have anything new to say to us. We'll know our histories. We'll have walked around our beliefs in daylight and have given each one a hard kick. We'll be the arbiters of our own lives.

Once we have explored ourselves in this way, we may become less tempted to do something that—though it may only actively interest a small part of the population—nevertheless sheds important light on our psychological vulnerability to the media: search for our name on the internet. When we put our name into a search engine to see what the media make of us—an action as foolish and as hard to resist as to search for ourselves in someone else's diary—we are implicitly revealing a belief that the vital truth about ourselves must in essence be out there rather than in here. They, the ones in digital space, will be the ones to decide whether we are good or bad, they will be the ones to weigh up whether our personal lives are tolerable, whether our partner is acceptable, whether our work is up to scratch and whether our morals are sound. Just one indication to the contrary, one blog post or nasty article in another direction, might be enough to throw us off balance and rock the foundations of our being.

But if we have explored our ideas for long enough, if we know our own lives from the inside, if we are fully in possession of the very worst things that could be said about us with reason, then what the search engine throws up will only ever manage to exert so much pain or assume so much significance. We will know in our-selves whether we are brilliant or depressing, we'll have made our peace with our flaws and temptations, we'll know how ugly or pretty we are, it'll be old news that we are, in areas, idiots or weirdos. Anything else will be random insanity and projection on the part of strangers wrestling with their own perturbances. We won't regul-arly have to check online, because there will be nothing the media can teach us about who we are—be it sad or admirable—that we have not already known about in our own well-charted minds for a long time.

Analyse the Role the Media Plays in Your Life

In a better world, the media would be reformed from the ground up. It would be institutionally geared towards looking for solutions, it would never inflame situations, it would be kind, it would highlight virtue, it would educate us in patience, hope and resilience, it would give us role models who were within reach; it would be genuinely trained on trying to improve society. It would be productive in its criticisms. In assessing those who had done wrong, it would be trained on rehabilitation rather than condemnation. It would be careful to render the world liveable.

Along the way, there might be a need for a Centre for the Victims of Trolling, a clinic where those who had been most badly manhandled by the mediatised world would be able to recover their strength, assess their traumas, understand the forces that had tried to destroy them and find a way back to a tolerable existence.

But we are all often victims of media even if we don't appear in it. Just by being its passive consumers, by letting it wake us up every morning, by allowing it to fill our feeds and irrigate our thoughts, we too can count among those it damages. It can help to turn us against one another and forget our good sense. It can sensationalise our emotions. Our days can be marred through its baiting and catcalls. We must be allowed to put a wall up between ourselves and hatred and unproductive partisanship. Learning to be careful around the media belongs at the heart of how to lead the more mentally balanced and tolerable future we deserve.

Picture Credits

p. 110   Josse Lieferinxe, *Saint Sebastian Interceding for the Plague Stricken,*1497–1499. Oil on wood, 81.8 cm × 55.4 cm. The Walters Art Museum, Baltimore, USA

p. 115   Michael Putland / Getty Images

p. 117   Bettmann / Getty Images

p. 119   Wojsyl / Wikimedia Commons (CC BY-SA 3.0)

p. 123   Émile Lévy, *Jules Barbey d'Aurevilly*, 1882 / Wikimedia Commons

p. 129   Benvenuto Cellini, *Salt Cellar*, c. 1540–1543. Gold, enamel, ebony, ivory, 28.5 cm × 21.5 cm × 26.3 cm. Kunsthistorisches Museum, Vienna, Austria. KHM-Museumsverband

p. 130   Benvenuto Cellini, *Bearded Man*, c. 1540–1543. Graphite on paper, 28.3 cm × 18.5 cm. Royal Library of Turin, Turin, Italy. Dantedellrosa / Wikimedia Commons (CC BY-SA 4.0)

p. 132   George M. Bergman / Wikimedia Commons (CC BY-SA 4.0)

p. 135   Tea Bowl with Hare's-Fur Decoration, 16th century. Stoneware with iron-oxide glaze; metal rim (Seto ware), 7.3 cm × 12.4 cm. Met Museum, New York, USA. H. O. Havemeyer Collection, Bequest of Mrs. H. O. Havemeyer, 1929. Accession Number: 29.100.234

p. 138   Zuma Press

P. 141   Eugène Delacroix, *Medea about to Kill her Children*, 1838. Oil on canvas, 260 cm × 165 cm. Palais des Beaux-Arts de Lille, Lille, France / Wikimedia Commons

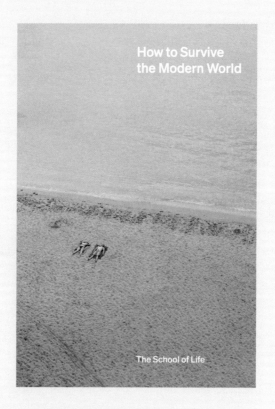

How to Survive
the Modern World

The School of Life

How To Survive the Modern World
Making sense of, and finding calm in, unsteady times

A guide to modern times that explores the challenges that living in the 21st century can pose to our mental well-being.

The modern world has brought us a range of extraordinary benefits and joys, including technology, medicine and transport. But it can also feel as though modern times have plunged us ever deeper into greed, despair and agitation. Seldom has the world felt more privileged and resource-rich yet also worried, blinkered, furious, panicked and self-absorbed.

This is the ultimate guide to navigating our unusual times. It identifies a range of themes that present acute challenges to our mental well-being. The book tackles our relationship to the news media, our ideas of love and sex, our assumptions about money and our careers, our attitudes to the natural world, our admiration for science and technology, our belief in individualism—and our suspicion of quiet and solitude.

The emphasis isn't just on understanding modern times but also on knowing how we can best relate to the difficulties these present. If modern times are (in part) something of a disease, this is both the diagnostic and the soothing, hope-filled cure.

ISBN   978-1-912891-53-5

£20.00 | $29.99

Insomnia

A GUIDE TO, AND CONSOLATION FOR,
THE RESTLESS EARLY HOURS

Insomnia

A guide to, and consolation for, the restless early hours

Guidance for the restless insomniac—providing comfort on even the longest of sleepless nights.

Not being able to sleep is deeply frightening. We panic about our ability to cope with the demands of the next day; we panic that we are panicking; the possibility of sleep recedes ever further as the clock counts down to another exhausted, irritable dawn.

Our societies have learnt to treat insomnia with the best-applied discipline we know: medicine—in particular, with pills powerful enough to wrestle consciousness into submission. But there are other things to do besides, or alongside, medicalising insomnia. We can reflect on our sleeplessness, define it to ourselves and others, try to understand where it springs from in human nature and speculate on what it might—in its own confused way—be trying to tell us.

This book is an eloquent guide to, and companion through, the long sleepless hours of the night. We come away from its soothing pages informed, consoled and armed with insights that will make us feel a lot less alone—as we wait for sleep, eventually, to come.

ISBN   978-1-9999179-7-5

£10.00 | $14.99

The School of Life is a global organisation helping people lead more fulfilled lives. It is a resource for helping us understand ourselves, for improving our relationships, our careers and our social lives—as well as for helping us find calm and get more out of our leisure hours. We do this through films, workshops, books, apps, gifts and community. You can find us online, in stores and in welcoming spaces around the globe.

Published in 2022 by The School of Life
First published in the USA in 2022
930 High Road, London, N12 9RT

Copyright © The School of Life 2022

Designed and typeset by Studio Katie Kerr
Printed in Latvia by Livonia

A proportion of this book has appeared online at
www.theschooloflife.com/thebookoflife

Every effort has been made to contact the copyright holders of
the material reproduced in this book. If any have been inadvertently overlooked, the publisher will be pleased
to make restitution at the earliest opportunity.

www.theschooloflife.com

ISBN 978-1-912891-88-7

10 9 8 7 6 5 4 3 2 1

MIX
Paper from
responsible sources
FSC® C002795